GATEWAYS TO GLORY

♦

DAN JARRARD

PublishAmerica
Baltimore

First printing

At the specific preference of the author, PublishAmerica allowed this work to remain exactly as the author intended, verbatim, without editorial input.

ISBN: 1-4241-4150-8
PUBLISHED BY PUBLISHAMERICA, LLLP
www.publishamerica.com
Baltimore

Printed in the United States of America

This book is affectionately dedicated to my four
"grand"children:
Christian, Brayson, Rebecca, and Jackson.
It is dedicated to them with an accompanying
prayer that as they travel the journey of life, each
threshold they encounter will be crossed with
integrity and lead them to an ever-increasing
awareness of the
"Gateways To Glory."
Grandpa Loves You!

Table of Contents

Introduction

The oldest continuing miracle is that concerning Revelation. This miracle is still in the process of unfolding – even to this hour. Because of this, the Old Testament is not to be discarded or disregarded, but rather is to be accepted, since Its intention was planned by God – whether concerning types, antitypes or realities, and should speak to us as Specific Truth.

Upon investigating the book of Nehemiah, it becomes clear that God's Spirit moved upon that writer to preserve intricate details of a special building project. The opening portion of the account portrays a scene of sadness, as Nehemiah received reports of the harsh days of trial and discouragement which had fallen upon those who had returned to Jerusalem from captivity. They had started the work of rebuilding the city of Jerusalem with great enthusiasm, but soon the enemy began to cause disturbance and the ministry of restoration was hindered. Not only had the temple services been disturbed, but the people were living in constant fear because the city walls still lay in ruins and so they felt unprotected.

Nehemiah allowed the report to affect him in a noticeable way as he harbored it in his mind and heart. After weeks of sleepless nights and care-filled days his countenance could no longer conceal the aching of his soul. Following a time of prayer, the Lord provided an occasion when the servant of God could share his concern with the king and ask, with courage, to be released from his palace duties so that he might travel to Jerusalem and be used of God to do a work of revival. He was granted his request.

When Nehemiah arrived at Jerusalem things were dismal and negative. Under his direction, the wall was given special attention due to its significance relative to the separation, protection, and inspiration to Israel. Within this wall, were inserted twelve gates – three on each of four sides, which reveal a balance in God's Plan Of Salvation. These gates may rightly be termed, **GATEWAYS TO GLORY**.

With a miraculous melody of praise emerging from his soul, Nehemiah was instrumental in inspiring the rebuilding of the gates of Jerusalem – gates of not mere wood or stone, but actually, **GATEWAYS TO GLORY**, which stood as a memorial-type to the Complete Plan Of Redemption.

Since the completion of those gates in the wall of Jerusalem, the skies have often been covered over with seeming blackness at various times in the history of mankind – and at each occurrence, there have always come forth those power-endued witnesses who asked, believed, and claimed God's ability to enable the faithful to overcome and emerge into the light of His Glory.

As a general rule, all of this Glory does not arrive at once, for there is no one-giant step to gain its full splendor. But one step at a time, the persistent Christian marches onward in grand parade form, finishing the course with victory to await the Resurrection Day Celebration.

As we share in the study of these **GATEWAYS TO GLORY**, I long for each of us to be enabled to become a "little Nehemiah" through the words and spirit of this presentation. My aspiration is that our Lord will grant that during this time together we might become united in both prayer and purpose, so that we can be led through the **GATEWAYS TO GLORY** and become more effective testimonies to the fact that: *"THE GOD OF HEAVEN, HE WILL PROSPER US,"* because we are *"HIS SERVANTS"* (Nehemiah 2:20).

Most Scripture Truths have at least a twofold meaning in regard to fulfillment: First, that of historical or local significance; Second, that of spiritual significance. For, *"all Scripture is given by inspiration of God, and is profitable for doctrine, for reproof, for correction, for instruction in righteousness"* (II Timothy 3:16). With this fact in mind and heart, let's proceed to the **FIRST GATE – THE SHEEP GATE.**

Chapter One

THE SHEEP GATE

"Then Eliashib the high priest rose up with his brethren the priests, and they builded the ***sheep gate****; they sanctified it, and set up the doors of it; even unto the tower of Meah they sanctified it, unto the tower of Hananeel. And next unto him builded the men of Jericho. And next to them builded Zaccur the son of Imri."*

(Nehemiah 3:1,2)

The **SHEEP GATE** was geographically located at the eastern end of the north wall and Spiritually Signifies the **initial work of Grace referred to as The New Birth.**

Throughout the Old Testament, lambs were sacrificially offered by man unto God as an external expression of an inward faith which looked forward in prophetic assurance to the finished work of *"the seed of woman"* (Genesis 3:15).

Most vividly, the account of the initial Passover established the lamb, and blood thereof, to be a memorial of redemption. For hundreds of years Israel had labored and despaired in the dark, burdensome clutches of Egyptian bondage – knowing only the growl of empty stomachs, pain of beaten backs, agony of negative thoughts, and catastrophe of broken spirits.

Yet, despite mountainous obstacles, God began to move – in accord with His Word, Will, and Way – to perform a miracle of giving a "new birth" to that band of slaves. And the first step to their glory must be through the **SHEEP GATE**.

One can almost sense the glow on the face of Moses as the message of God penetrated to the soul of that "drawn out one." Listen to not only the words, but thrill to the Spiritual Significance as the command was received: *". . . they shall take to them every man a lamb . . . a lamb for an house . . . your lamb shall be without blemish, a male of the first year . . . and they shall take of the blood, and Strike it on the two side posts on the upper door post of the houses, wherein they shall eat it . . . For I will pass through the land of Egypt this night . . . and the blood shall be to you for a token . . . and when I see the blood, I will pass over you . . . and this day shall be unto you a memorial . . . "* (Exodus 12:3-14).

What an exuberant joy it must have been for those believers to walk out of the tenacious grasp of Egypt, and into the light of glorious freedom. A nation had been "reborn" because of faith in the God of the lamb and its blood.

To the sincere student of Scripture, there can surely be no doubt that the **SHEEP GATE** Experience typifies the office and administration of Jesus the Christ as our Saviour, and serves as the foundation for all who will accept. This thread of truth stitches together every jot and tittle, confirming the prophetic insight of Isaiah: *". . . He is brought as a Lamb to the slaughter, and as a Sheep before her shearers is dumb, so He openeth not His mouth"* (Isaiah 53:7).

Many years before the first Passover, in obedience to the test of God, Abraham and Isaac marched upward, toward the summit of Mount Moriah. With the eyes of Heaven focused in their direction the young lad *"spoke unto Abraham, his father, and said, my father . . . Behold the fire and wood: but where is the lamb for a burnt offering?"* Without breaking his stride, the "friend of God" looked down upon the expression of his love, and with assurance of soul confidently answered, *"My son, **GOD WILL PROVIDE HIMSELF A LAMB . . .**"* (Genesis 22:1-14).

Through the centuries the anxiety of Isaac's question picked up momentum: **"WHERE IS THE LAMB?"** But, *"when the fullness of the time was come, God sent forth His Son, made of a woman,* *made under the law, to redeem them that were under the law, that we might receive the adoption of sons"* (Galatians 4:4,5).

Many times John the Baptist was questioned as to whether he was the Expected One, and each time he answered in the negative. One day his eyes must have sparkled and his pulse quickened as he looked up and saw Jesus walking in his direction. John raised his voice so all could hear and spoke the answer to Isaac's question: *"**BEHOLD THE LAMB OF GOD**, WHO TAKETH AWAY THE SIN OF THE WORLD"* (John 1:29).

Jesus is *"THE LAMB SLAIN FROM THE FOUNDATION OF THE WORLD"* (Revelation 13:8), and declares the beauty of the **SHEEP GATE** so aptly in John 10:7 – *". . . I am the door . . ."*

When an individual walks through this blood-purchased passage, *"he* (or she) *is a new creation; old things are passed away; behold, all things are become new"* (II Corinthians 5:17); and immediately this new creature is adopted as a baby lamb, a spiritual sheep, into the fold of a Loving Father God.

To believe in the Inspiration of God's Word is to avail ourselves to veins of golden truth and oceans of clear facts that enhance our understanding the deep-seeded implications of texts and contexts. The meanings of Biblical names add insight to their respective circumstances and weight to the surrounding environment. Names point out the character and personality traits of individuals, while, at the same time, spelling the drama of unfolding events in relation to the Plan of God.

The names of those who labored on the **SHEEP GATE** serve to intensify the Glory of God as the respective definitions are noted.

"Eliashib" was the high priest during the time of Nehemiah's ministry, and his name means "God will restore." For years the Jews had been bound by complacent, negative attitudes and thoughts, getting nothing of real importance accomplished on the wall of Jerusalem. Immediately after the positive exercise of Nehemiah's faith and dynamic promise that *"God will prosper us"* (2:20), the high priest, whose name exclaims the provision of God's Restorative Ability, is seen arising from his position to lead the way to glory.

When the world was at a dark moment and it seemed that the crowning work of God's creation would be cast into a state of total apostasy, the High Priest of Heaven – Jesus, Whose Name means "God Will Save," arose from His position of Deity and condescended to the place of Bethlehem and was born of a virgin. He walked for 33 ½ years upon the earth, being tempted in all points as we are; was crucified on an old rugged cross, buried in a cold, damp, dark, dismal tomb, and came forth on the third day, waving the keys of death and the grave in the face of Satan, exclaiming to the world that He had gained the victory and *"whosoever will"* might walk through the **SHEEP GATE** and be saved.

It must also be noted that *"the priests"* were involved in the glory of this gate. These priests represent those who have received a definite call to minister unto needy mankind. God has chosen redeemed man to echo the story of salvation and all Christians are constituted as a *"kingdom of priests"* (I Peter 2:5,9; Revelation 1:6).

Just before His Ascension, Christ issued the missionary commission to all generations: *"Feed My lambs and My sheep"* (John 21:15-17).

After the **SHEEP GATE** had been dedicated, *"the doors of it were set up."* While it is true that salvation is freely available to *"whosoever will,"* the willing one has to align to the Way of God. The New Birth is not gained by the keeping of ceremonial or social traditions of men, for Jesus has declared of Himself, *"I am the Way, the Truth, and the Life; no man cometh unto the Father, but by Me . . . Verily, verily I say unto you, he that entereth not by the door into the sheepfold, but climbeth up some other way, the same is a thief and a robber . . . I am the door of the sheep"* (John 14:6;10:1,7). Indeed, we can be thankful to God for the safeguards of Calvary.

Connected to the **SHEEP GATE** were two towers: One was *"Meah,"* which means "Hundred"; the other was *"Hananeel,"* which means "God is gracious."

The tower of Meah establishes that there is nothing lacking nor half-hearted about the gift of salvation. God does not save an individual partly, but when a person accepts Jesus as Saviour, he or she instantly becomes a *"child of God"* (John 1:12). This does not mean that there will not be further concessions and surrenders on the part of the newly converted one to the Will of God, but it does mean that the believer has 100% of God's Power at his or her disposal if faith is exercised and growth in grace and knowledge is desired.

The tower of Hananeel captures the New Testament expression of Paul to the church at Rome, *"the goodness of God leadeth thee to repentance"* (Romans 2:4). The New Birth cannot be earned by good works, but rather is freely given on the basis of Divine Grace to anyone who will ask and receive by faith.

Since the initial transgression of Adam, the propensity of all mankind has been to delve into the forbidden areas, thus bringing about suffering and remorse. And had it not been for the Infinite Goodness of God, the world and all its inhabitants would have been destroyed during such catastrophic events as the flood. However, a Promise had been made to Adam and God was and is as good as His Word. How Good God Is, to allow beams of Divine Goodness to lead individuals to a saving relationship with Him! Indeed, How Good He Is! To put up with so much of our frail thrashings and then accept us as His own – providing everything we need when we allow His Graciousness to both surround and penetrate to the deepest crevice of our being.

"Next unto the high priest builded the men of Jericho." The phrase "next unto" literally means "at his hand." Communion and unity seem to flow from this phrase with great expectancy. There is something about the New Birth that breaks across all lines and barriers, tongues and nations, races and creeds – thus establishing men and women on a common plateau of thanksgiving and praise for a supernatural miracle of being made joint heirs in Christ.

"Jericho" means "fragrance." This is one of the many benefits and characteristics of the New Birth. There is no beauty in a father who beats a child to the brink of death. There is no beauty in a young girl whose body is sold for a few moments of lustful pleasure. There is no beauty or blissful fragrance to sin and sinning.

No wonder David penned the words of a new song, as the fragrance of reconciliation to God settled an old account. With raised voice he sang in a melodious tone: *"God brought me up also out of an horrible pit, out of the miry clay, and set my feet upon a rock, and established my goings"* (Psalms 40:2).

When Christ, The Anointed One, enters the heart of an individual, a radical change occurs. The stale odor of sin is removed and in its stead is placed a fragrance of Divine Origin. How lovely and thrilling it is to witness the change in an individual as Jesus begins to reign in a life; for now that person begins to give forth the aroma of Heaven's Perfume made from the Lily of the Valley and the Rose of Sharon. Listen as the redeemed one is described by Solomon: *"How much better is thy love than wine: And the fragrance of thine ointments than all spices: Thy lips, O my spouse, drop like the honeycomb; honey and milk are under thy tongue, and the scent of thy garments is like the fragrance of Lebanon"* (Song Of Solomon 4:10,11).

"And next to the men of Jericho builded Zaccur." Zaccur means "thoughtful." Not only does the New Birth bring about a change of heart, but it also alters and re-channels the process of thinking. The mind is a powerful and intricate computer, and inseparable from the spiritual makeup of man. The Bible is most emphatic in stating that a carnal mind produces evil thoughts, which lead to enmity against God.

It is to be realized that many do not recognize the effects produced by thinking. We speak of doing something before thinking about it, but in reality, every word and act is more or less the result of a previous thought at one time or another. A person is really no better than the thoughts, and deeds are only thoughts which have been hung out where they can be readily seen. The old adage, "We will not be hanged for our thoughts," is poor security; for our thinking fixes our course, and this leads to our destiny.

But thank God, multitudes can testify to the fact that the **SHEEP GATE** has wrought a transformation of their thought pattern. When the Mind of the Master becomes the Master of one's mind (I

Corinthians 2:16), God has made a positive promise to keep that person in *"perfect peace"* (Isaiah 26:3).

Many who have harbored ill thoughts about God, others, and themselves have discovered the multiplied joy of "thoughtfulness" after allowing the New Birth Experience to become a way of life. With detailed expressiveness, Mark records an incident that still warms the soul of a sincere Bible student. It is found in Mark 5.

As Jesus stepped from a boat onto the shore of the Gadarenes, a man whose life was tormented by Satan confronted Him. Demon possession had caused this sin-laden individual to flee his home and take up a hermit style of existence among the tombs of a local cemetery.

The depraved state of this man was far advanced, but Jesus has never met a case He could not both diagnose and cure. Here they stood – a sinful creature on one side of the "gate" and The Saving Christ on the other side. With Love Of Divine Origin, Jesus administered a miracle of Re-Birth. Demons fled and the soul of that liberated man began to offer praise of thanksgiving for his newfound peace.

Word quickly spread and the multitude came to witness for themselves if the report was true. To their amazement they saw the man not only in a calm, serene sitting position, but *"clothed, and in his right mind"* (Mark 5:15). Thoughts of Glory radiated from his countenance as a result of having walked through the **SHEEP GATE**.

Men, women, and youth are still being converted today as they individually hear and hearken to the Voice of The Great Shepherd as He tenderly beckons, *"Behold, I stand at the door and knock; if any man hear My Voice, and open the door, I will come in to him, and will sup with him, and he with Me"* (Revelation 3:20).

To walk through the **SHEEP GATE** of Salvation is to be ushered onto a Glory Road that will lead all the way to the Heaven of God's Presence.

Chapter Two

THE FISH GATE

"But the fish gate did the sons of Hassenaah build, who also laid the beams thereof, and set up the doors thereof, the locks thereof, and the bars thereof. And next unto them repaired Meremoth the son of Urijah, the son of Koz. And next unto them repaired Meshullam the son of Berechiah, the son of Meshezabeel. And next unto them repaired Zadok the son of Baana. And next unto them the Tekoites repaired; but their nobles put not their necks to the work of their Lord."

(Nehemiah 3:3-5)

This gate seems to have been located in the middle of the northern wall near the fish market where the Tyrians sold their fish. The Spiritual Significance of this gate is that it **represents the ministry of Soulwinning.**

Immediately, upon walking through the **SHEEP GATE** and experiencing the Saving Grace of Jesus Christ, the newly converted one witnesses a strong desire to share with someone else the good news of what has taken place in his or her life. Soulwinning is not only a high privilege, it is an imperative obligation to tell others about the Wonderful Saviour Who has enabled the believer to pass from death into life.

Christians are to bring forth spiritual children. Even as the commission was made, in the physical, to the first man and woman (*"Be fruitful, and multiply"* – Genesis 1:28), we, as disciples of Christ, are charged in the spiritual to make disciples of all men. Just as the natural outcome of a union of a man and woman is that of children, even so should the supernatural outcome of a union of Christ and a believer be that of giving birth to those with whom contact is made.

Even as Andrew brought Peter, Philip brought Nathanael, and the woman of Samaria brought forth many to the knowledge of Jesus, it is the responsibility and honor of us who have entered into this blessed relationship to cast both hooks and nets into the disturbed sea of peoples that we may be thrilled in becoming soulwinners.

God may not have called us all to be renown evangelists or pastors of large churches, but He has called us all, each and every one, to be witnesses of His Son. *"And Jesus, walking by the sea of Galilee, saw two brethren, Simon called Peter, and Andrew his brother, casting a net into the sea: for they were fishers. And He saith unto them, Follow Me, and I will make you fishers of men"* (Matthew 4:18,19).

The **FISH GATE** contained *"beams."* According to the dictionary, a beam is one of the principal or main pieces in a construction that lies across the walls and serves not only to support, but also to balance the building.

There should be nothing of an unbalanced nature concerning Soulwinning, and how can such a guarantee be maintained? Jesus gave the answer: *"Follow Me."* Christ is the Foundation, Support, and Balance of this important gate and to *"follow"* Him is to be led in a manner that will afford ample opportunities to witness in a spirit that will promote Christianity, rather than bring a reproach upon it.

Some are of the opinion that to be an effective soulwinner one has to attend Bible College or Seminary and learn the one, two, threes of presentation. While an education of such measure will certainly contribute much, it is not the fundamental foundation upon which Soulwinning must be launched.

To be an effective soulwinner, one only needs to do what comes natural after experiencing a tremendous blessing – SHARE – and Jesus has promised that He *"will make you fishers of men."* The promise to the "young lamb" is that Jesus will accomplish His Will as we *"follow"* Him.

"Doors, locks, and bars" were also part of the **FISH GATE** makeup. These valuable implements of hardware serve to represent the stability, strength, and security of the soulwinner.

Testimonial witness for Christ is to be regarded as a constant duty. *"Then they that feared the Lord spake often one to another; and the Lord hearkened, and heard it, and a book of remembrance was written before Him for them that feared the Lord, and that thought upon His Name"* (Malachi 3:16).

One is not to give witness of being a Christian just when he or she feels like it, but rather is to be as an established door, ready to open to the wayfaring stranger with radiant readiness. It is one thing to stand in the midst of fellow Christians and witness for the Lord, but it is quite a different matter to hand a Bible tract or begin a witnessing conversation to a complete stranger while riding aboard an elevator, rising to the fourteenth floor of a building. Peter was inspired to write these words in I Peter 3:15 – *"But sanctify the Lord God in your hearts: and be ready always to give an answer to every man that asketh you a reason of the hope that is in you with meekness and fear."*

No soulwinner is promised an easy road, but there is a Divine Assurance that, in the presence of the scoffer, Jesus and His Holy Spirit will give the necessary strength to stand and proclaim the Way of Excellence. Hebrews 13:5,6—*". . . I will never leave thee, nor forsake thee. So that we may boldly say, The Lord is my Helper, and I will not fear what man shall do unto me."*

Though multitudes have given their bodies as martyred vessels, the strength of Christ has relieved all physical and spiritual fear. One of the most dynamic soulwinners has to have been the apostle Paul. He displayed magnificent strength as he lived the **FISH GATE** life.

Though stones may be cast in the direction of the sincere Christian witness, he or she can experience the glow of Stephen, as he looked in the realm of Spiritual Security and exclaimed, *"I see Jesus."* There has not been a weapon invented which can harm the balanced soulwinner until God so allows. Just as the security of God was manifest in behalf of past soulwinners, even so it will be extended to the contemporary soulwinner, in accord with the Will of God: *"touch not Mine anointed"* (I Chronicles 16:22).

Even as the hedge was around Job and the horses and chariots were about Elisha, *"the angel of the Lord encampeth round about those that fear Him, and delivereth them"* (Psalms 34:7), until the faithful witness has finished his or her labor and is ready to await the resurrection to a Heavenly Reward. Indeed, there is stability, strength, and security available to the soulwinner who is persuaded of Christ's Ministry.

Five groups of people labored on the **FISH GATE** and each contributed to its completion. The Spiritual Significance of the Biblical meaning of their names, in relation to Soulwinning, is both enlightening and enthralling.

1. First, were the *"sons of Hassenaah."* Hassenaah means "pointed." The sincere soulwinner must be aware that every person is different, and thus, what is the right approach to one, may not be adequate for another. Here is where wisdom and tact are so important.

According to the dictionary, tact is "quick appreciation of what is proper, fitting, or right; the mental ability of doing and saying the right thing at the right time so as not to unjustly offend or anger." Tact has been referred to as the pointed life of the five senses: it is the open eye, the quick ear, the discerning taste, the keen smell, and the lively touch.

Those who spend much time fishing soon learn the value of knowing what kinds of bait and the proper methods to use in catching different kinds of fish. There is a great deal of difference in fishing for bass and fishing for trout. Isaiah, the grand Old Testament soulwinner, gave tremendous insight into his effectiveness when he made the statement recorded in Isaiah 50:4. *"The Lord God hath given me the tongue of the learned, that I should know how to speak a word in season to him that is weary . . .* "Philip, a New Testament evangelist, gives a shining example of pointed, not dull, dealings with an individual in need (Acts 8). He did not ignorantly blurt out to the Ethiopian eunuch, "Are you a Christian? If not, you are in danger of destruction." But rather, he took careful, pointed aim at the soul of that hungry, thirsty one and tactfully asked, *"Understandest thou what thou readest?"* Thus the door was willingly opened by the responsive sinner and Philip became a soulwinner on the dusty road from Jerusalem to Gaza. In the midst of that desert, the Ethiopian was led into the Stream Of Living Water.

It is possible to do a right thing in a wrong way, so a Christian should be pointed and tactful in order to assure that wisdom manifests itself in each Soulwinning endeavor.

2. *"And next unto them repaired Meremoth."* Meremoth means "heights." The world lays bleeding and ravaged by sin, and a Christian who has never experienced the high honor of leading a ragged, needful soul into the Glory of The New Birth is selling himself or herself short.

Soulwinning should not only be the heart-throb of the church, as a corporate unit, it must also be the motivation of individual members of the Body of Christ. Only as we *"work while it is day"* (John 9:4) can we expect to be strong and increase in spirit, as well as number. When Soulwinning zeal dwindles, when the excitement of being a child of The King subsides, when the fire of the **FISH GATE** dims its radiant glow, the professing Christian is in grave danger of losing his or her spiritual victory. If you were to place your arm in a sling and refuse to use it, what would soon happen? It would become weak and useless, poisoning the system of the body function.

The church family or individual Christian who becomes sterile and ceases to produce spiritual offspring soon loses not only identity, but also existence.

The **FISH GATE** immediately follows the **SHEEP GATE** so as to allow the new convert to share The Christ with someone else. The thrill of being a soulwinner is an elevating occasion. What greater joy could the Christian have than knowing and experiencing James 5:20? *"Let him know, that he which converteth the sinner from the error of his way, shall save a soul from death, and shall hide a multitude of sins."*

Notice the height to which Daniel equates the soulwinner. *"And they that be wise shall shine as the brightness of the firmament; and they that turn many to righteousness as the stars for ever and ever"* (Daniel 12:3).

Heights of blissful grandeur await the soulwinner. Our Heavenly Father longs for each of His children to witness this blessed joy.

3. *"And next unto them repaired Meshullam."* Meshullam means "a friend, allied." Within the Spiritual Significance of this name is contained a twofold application.

First, that of friend, or contact. Jesus gave us a Personal example of this truth. Christ did not isolate Himself in some mountainous hut and abstain from contact with society, but throughout the Gospels He is seen both touching and being touched by sinners. The self-righteous, pompous religionists of that time did not understand and thus repeatedly accused the Son of God with unholy actions, but He swerved not from His commitment to be *"a Friend that sticketh closer than a brother"* (Psalms 18:24), to all mankind.

The person outside God's family does not need someone to pass by on the other side or place a foot of scorn upon the wounded soul, but rather needs to be ministered unto by one who is of a friendly nature, exemplifying the spirit of the good Samaritan (Luke 10:30-37).

To be a friend of Jesus is to be friendly to those who need Him as Saviour. Many have braved the storms of raging seas, the humid climate of torrid jungles, the barren lands of heathen tribes, that they might show that Christ is the answer to the need of man.

Just because one has walked through the **SHEEP GATE** does not mean that now is the time to relax. There is a work to be done and the ministry of being a friend to the friendless may well serve to lead them through the **SHEEP GATE** as well.

Second, the meaning of Meshullam signifies that of "allied or unity." There is power in a unified, allied Soulwinning effort. No man is an island unto himself, nor is any man so intellectually equipped so as not to need the profitable experiences of those who have blazed trails amidst the wilderness of sin in days gone by.

Some have walked through the **SHEEP GATE** and unto the **FISH GATE**, endeavoring to conquer the world as single, separate, segregated dynamos, and have fallen flat on their backs. While it is true that a new convert can share his or her personal testimony of what Christ has done in their respective lives on a one to one basis with a great deal of success, Jesus also saw the need of togetherness when loftier Soulwinning campaigns are to be launched. Mark 6:7—*"And He called unto Him the twelve, and began to send them forth by two and two; and gave them power over unclean spirits."*

Every new convert to Christianity needs to be taken under the spiritual wings of a mature, enthusiastic, concerned soldier of the Cross. If nothing else, the new Christian needs to be aware that someone is allied with him or her in prayer that opportunities may be opened to witness and that these doors will be entered into with a positive assurance that a fellow believer is spiritually there with him or her. Every Paul needs an Ananias, and every Timothy needs a Paul.

A famous statesman once said, "United we stand, divided we fall." The church must allow the cords of love and the strings of concern to ally us into a triumphant organism, bound and determined to win the lost at any cost.

For too long we have permitted petty prejudices and meager means to disembody one of the most influential elements at God's Disposal for spreading the Good News. Let the old anthem challenge us continually to "Stand Up, Stand Up For Jesus" like a mighty army, marching under the Banner of the Lord to meet the magnitude of our mission; sustaining one another as did Aaron and Hur unto Moses (Exodus 17:8-16), so that humanity may witness that we are on business for the King.

4. *"And next unto them repaired Zadok."* Zadok means "righteous." In order to effectively bring others to Christ, one must first have already come to Him and be walking *"in the light, as He is in the light"* (I John 1:1-7). The Gift of God does not need to be exaggerated, but merely expressed in the right manner at the right time.

Jesus was most emphatic when He said, *"First cast the beam out of thine own eye, and then shalt thou see clearly to cast the mote out of thy brother's eye"* (Matthew 7:5), for, *". . . can the blind lead the blind? Shall they not both fall into the ditch?"* (Luke 6:39).

We must never try to tell someone else how they should live if we ourselves are guilty of failing to measure to the spiritual statue we are claiming. Only eternity will unfold exactly how much harm has been committed, both internally and externally, by those who followed the philosophy, "Do as I say, not as I do." The Christian soulwinner is to be an open book, *"known and read of all men"* (II Corinthians 3:2).

We need to pray that the Lord will send laborers unto the harvest field of ripe souls – laborers who are genuinely motivated, not by their own self-righteousness, but by the Righteousness of God. Laborers, like John the Baptist, whose Soulwinning efforts paved the path for the "Beloved Son," as he willingly pointed men unto the Way Of Salvation, living humbly and moving in this truth, *"He must increase, but I must decrease"* (John 3:30).

Indeed, *"all our righteousnesses are as filthy rags"* (Isaiah 64:6), but the born-again soulwinner who is keeping the spirit of the **FISH GATE**, also has the blessed consolation of I Corinthians 1:30,31 – *"But of Him are ye in Christ Jesus, Who of God is made unto us wisdom, and righteousness, and sanctification, and redemption: That, according as it is written, He that glorieth, let him glory in the Lord."*

5. *"And next unto them the Tekoites repaired."* Tekoites means "trumpets." Repeatedly through the Scriptures the trumpet is used as an instrument of announcement because of its clear, distinct ability to penetrate to the inner particles and stir the physical and emotional awareness of the hearer.

To be a Christian is the most important position a person can attain unto in this life, and one does not have to wear a neon sign of flashing letters for the world to discover something of distinct difference in the believer's life; for as Christians we do not have to put on a show. Jesus has already declared that we are the light of the world and as such, we are to simply let our light so shine before others; not hiding under a cover, but on a candlestick, that they may see our good works and glorify our Father, Who is in Heaven (Matthew 5:13-16).

To Timothy, the young man in the faith, Paul addressed a most instructive charge in II Timothy 1:8. *"Be not thou therefore ashamed of the testimony of our Lord, nor of me His prisoner, but be thou partaker of the afflictions of the gospel according to the power of God."*

Christians should be the happiest, most communicative people upon the earth. Every thing one needs to be happy and victorious is at our grasp, if we ask in faith according to the Word of God. And we should be blaring like a trumpet, if you will, from lip and life, with the message of the "Old, Old Story Of Jesus And His Love."

God is not looking for a silent partner, but He is looking, even in your direction and mine, for a person who will *"make up the hedge, and stand in the gap before Me* (God) *for the land . . . "* (Ezekiel 22:30).

Like a finely tuned trumpet, placed to the Divine Lips of The Holy Spirit, the soulwinner's melodious tone needs to go forth: *"Come unto* (Jesus), *all ye that labor and are heavy laden, and* (He) *will give you rest"* (Matthew 11:28).

What a lovely portrait of the soulwinner is painted within the expressions of these constructive names who worked on the **FISH GATE**. However, there is a danger of immense proportion which needs to be considered; for verse five ends with these mournful words, *"but their nobles put not their necks to the work of the Lord."*

These nobles were seasoned veterans who had gained positions of noteworthy leadership yet they were failing God, their fellow man, and themselves while maintaining posts of prestige. They should have been the first to the task of God's work, but they thought themselves to have outgrown the necessity of actual labor. How disturbing this could have been to those whose hands were busy at the **FISH GATE**.

Sad to report, there are leaders within the rank and file of church denominations and officers of local churches who have, unconsciously no doubt, fallen into the mold of those nobles and have come forth as unprofitable leaders.

The life and growth of the church do not reside in programs and committees. The future of the church rests on our willingness to return to the basic principle of reproduction – **SOULWINNING**.

Little wonder new converts often do not sense the urgency of walking through the **FISH GATE**; when they become aware that some local churches have failed to exert the energies of "adding daily" (Acts 2:47;16:5) to the number through the power of God's Holy Spirit.

It is not enough to be "evangelical" – we must be "evangelistic." The evangelical church is like those nobles – a reservoir of water without a pipe leading anywhere. If an unbeliever goes to the trouble and bother of going to it and climbing the embankment, he or she can get a good drink. The evangelistic church is a reservoir of pure water with pipes leading to every part of the community and does not wait for an invitation to share a Message Of Hope.

Let us ever be a people convicted of the importance of the **FISH GATE** so that we may be ever discovering and experiencing the elevating ecstasy of being a soulwinner.

Chapter Three

THE OLD GATE

"Moreover the ***old gate*** *repaired Jehoiada the son of Paseah, and Meshullam the son of Besodeiah; they laid the beams thereof, and set up the doors thereof, and the locks thereof, and the bars thereof. And next unto them repaired Melatiah the Gibeonite, and Jadon the Meronothite, the men of Gibeon, and of Mizpah, unto the throne of the governor on this side the river. Next unto him repaired Uzziel the son of Harhaiah, of the goldsmiths. Next unto him also repaired Hananiah the son of one of the apothecaries, and they fortified Jerusalem unto the broad wall. And next unto them repaired Rephaiah the son of Hur, the ruler of the half part of Jerusalem. And next unto them repaired Jedaiah the son of Harumaph, even over against his house. And next unto him repaired Hattush the son of Hashabniah. Malchijah the son of Harim, and Hashub the son of Pahathmoab, repaired the other piece, and the tower of the furnaces. And next unto him repaired Shallum the son of Halohesh, the ruler of the half part of Jerusalem, he and his daughters."*

(Nehemiah 3:6-12)

This gate seems to have been geographically located in the northwest section of the city wall, and the Spiritual Significance is that it **represents the establishing of systematic Bible Study.**

The Christian who fails to read the Scripture can never expect to be excited about or stable in his or her religious worship and service.

The most important, the most revealing book in existence is the Bible.

Those who neglect to walk through the **OLD GATE** spend their energies in a fashion which is not as productive as it could be. They never seem to be able to fully get off the ground and discover the thrill of soaring above the clouds of gloom, skipping above the mountains of despair, and leaping across the oceans of negative attitudes.

Someone has stated about God's Holy Word: "Worse than the attack of Its enemies is the neglect of Its friends." Every Christian needs to know the Bible and every church needs members who allow themselves to consume a balanced diet of solid Bible Truth that will usher them into the Glory of growth *"in grace and knowledge"* (II Peter 3:18).

Solomon, a man endowed with much wisdom, was very explicit in diagnosing the problem of why many choose to ignore God's command relative to the **OLD GATE**: *"much study,"* he penned in Ecclesiastes 12:12, *"is a weariness of the flesh."* The carnal nature of man had rather watch four hours of television than spend one hour in profitable searching of the Scriptures.

We should never allow anyone to convince us that study is easy. It is very demanding—mentally and physically, but oh how rewarding it is to the spirit. Very little good ever comes easy. There is a price to be paid and one must exercise strict discipline of body and mind to defeat the trickery of Satan, who tells us we are just too tired, do not have sufficient time, or not educated enough to perform our Christian duty of study.

Every Covenant Age has been challenged to earnestly read and study the Word of the Lord. Bible study has never been an option to the child of God; it has always been a command to be followed if true delight is to be enjoyed.

Moses, who was taught in the knowledge of Egyptian intellect and spent many years studying at the feet of heathen teachers, knew the value of God's Word. Used as an instrument to lay the groundwork for the Old Testament, Moses was permitted to look through the prophetic telescope and see that Israel would stray to the place of desiring a king in order to be like other nations. Aware that the people of God would be greatly endangered at such a time, Moses was inspired to encourage, in Deuteronomy 17:18,19 – *"And it shall be, when he sitteth upon the throne of his kingdom, that he shall write him a copy of this law in a book out of that which is before the priests the Levites: And it shall be with him, and he shall read therein all the days of his life: that he may learn to fear the LORD his God, to keep all the words of this law and these statutes, to do them."*

As Isaiah cast a reflective look backward on the close of the Old Covenant era and at the same time caught a glorious glimpse into the New Covenant era, he gave this noteworthy command found in Isaiah 34:16 – *"Seek ye out of the book of the Lord, and read . . ."*

Immediately, at the dawn of the New Covenant era, Jesus set the pace and pattern for continued **OLD GATE** practice. Listen as the Son of God issued not an option, but a command: *"Search the scriptures; for in them ye think ye have eternal life: and they are they which testify of Me"* (John 5:39). He Who was fully aware of the Old Covenant stipulation, did not change the course to be followed – He only added further weight and verity to the fact that Scripture Study is not only expedient, but also enlightening.

Paul was perhaps the most outstanding of apostolic adherents to the rigors of intellectual pursuit. For years he had sat at the feet of the renown, respected Gamaliel and had been well versed in the necessity of keeping aglow the flames of reading. No wonder God chose this man to be used in such a noteworthy fashion; for Paul was not ashamed to urge the converts under his ministry to apply themselves to the challenge of Scripture Study.

With stable spirit, Paul wrote words which not only stirred Timothy to the task of study, but words which have ignited scores of others through the centuries to apply themselves to Bible Study. I Timothy 4:11-16 – *"These things command and teach. Let no man despise thy youth; but be thou an example of the believers, in word, in conversation, in charity, in spirit, in faith, in purity. Till I come, give attendance to reading, to exhortation, to doctrine. Neglect not the gift that is in thee, which was given thee by prophecy, with the laying on of the hands of the presbytery. Meditate upon these things; give thyself wholly to them; that thy profiting may appear to all. Take heed unto thyself, and unto the doctrine; continue in them: for in doing this thou shalt both save thyself, and them that hear thee."*

The Christian needs to be a student of many areas of knowledge so as to be a well-balanced individual, but the main course of a quest must be that concerning Biblical Belief: *"Study to shew thyself approved unto God, a workman that needeth not to be ashamed, rightly dividing the word of truth. But shun profane and vain babblings: for they will increase unto more ungodliness. And their word will eat as doth a canker: of whom is Hymenaeus and Philetus; Who concerning the truth have erred, saying that the resurrection is past already; and overthrow the faith of some. Nevertheless the foundation of God standeth sure, having this seal, The Lord knoweth them that are His. And, Let every one that nameth the name of Christ depart from iniquity"* (II Timothy 2:15-19).

The Christian must ever proclaim, as a ready example: The Bible Is Worthy Of Our Study.

Now let's continue our quest for Truth as we notice the Spiritual Significance depicted in each of the twelve groups of personalities who labored on the important structure of the **OLD GATE**.

First, there was *"Jehoiada,"* whose name means "Jehovah knoweth." Theological circles tag the descriptive word of "Omniscience" to be one of the attributes of God. This word simply means that God knows everything about everything and has never had to learn anything.

To the Council at Jerusalem, James reminded, *"Known unto God are all His works from the beginning of the world"* (Acts 15:18). David penned additional insight in Psalms 147:5 – *"Great is our Lord, and of great power: His understanding is infinite."* Isaiah wrote that God has *"declared the end from the beginning"* (Isaiah 46:10).

Jesus stated, in Matthew 6:8 – *"Your Father knoweth what things ye have need of,"* and because God has always known what man has needed to give direction and purpose to life, He chose His Word to be an Expressive Gift to supply a guiding light amidst a world of darkness.

Some may have played the game of gossip at one time or another. In this game, a phrase or sentence is thought of and whispered into the ear of a person sitting next to you. That person, in turn, whispers to another, and thus the process continues until the last person has received the transmission. It is always quite amusing to hear the end result and how it often fails even to remotely resemble the beginning message.

The human mind is subject to not only the lapse of proper function from time to time, but also may be tempted by Satan to forget certain things which would interrupt his devilish schemes. Thus God knew that the best way to insure a safe conveying of His Message to man was through the medium of the Written Word.

In I Corinthians 2:16, Paul, in writing about the Revelation of God, says: *"For who hath known the mind of the Lord, that he may instruct Him? But we have the mind of Christ."* The Word is God's Mental Expression of His Will for mankind and the Christian is admonished with this counsel, found in Isaiah 46:8-10 – *"Remember this, and shew yourselves men: bring it again to mind, O ye transgressors. Remember the former things of old: for I am God, and there is none else; I am God, and there is none like Me, Declaring the end from the beginning, and from ancient times the things that are not yet done, saying, My counsel shall stand, and I will do all My pleasure."*

It should be noted that Jehoiada had a co-laborer in his ministry, he being *"Meshullam,"* whose name means "allied." What a marvelous transmittal of Spiritual Truth is here portrayed.

The Bible is without error and Christians can rest assured that *"every word of God is pure"* (Proverbs 30:5). David stood on the promises of Holy Communication as he wrote to the chief musician, *"the words of the Lord are pure words, like silver tested* (tried) *in a furnace of earth, purified seven times"* (Psalms 12:6).

The Bible has been dissected by some of the keenest minds in history, has been placed under the most powerful microscopes of critical analysis – in hopes of finding just one place where God contradicts Himself, and every attempt has failed. God's Word is allied. It is Stitched by the Holiness of God The Father, Bound by the Love Of God The Son, and Published by God The Holy Spirit.

"And next unto them repaired Melatiah," whose name means "Jehovah hath delivered." Because of the unity of Scripture, we are convinced of II Peter 1:20,21. *"Knowing this first, that no prophecy of the scripture is of any private interpretation. For the prophecy came not in old time by the will of man: but holy men of God spake as they were moved by the Holy Ghost."*

The FORTY-PLUS men whom God chose and qualified to do this work, spoke and wrote as they were inspired of God. God's Holy Spirit is the Bible's Author, and yet, God also used human instrumentality. In his role as a transmitter of a Divine Message, each prophet stood under the special anointing of God's Holy Spirit. This does not mean that they were mechanical robots of penmanship, but it does denote that God employed the attention, the investigation, the memory, the logic – all the faculties of the writers, so that each was enabled to speak and write with accuracy.

Each individual was guided to choose specific materials, speeches of others, imperial decrees, and genealogies relative to God's Plan Of Salvation. From the Divine side, God's Spirit delivered, through men, clearly and faithfully that which He wished to communicate. From the human side, the Bible was written by men using human languages, figures of speech and making references to human emotions, ideas, concepts, and imagery.

This cardinal truth of Christianity must be accepted. The fact of inspiration is stated most emphatically in II Timothy 3:16. *"All Scripture is given* (delivered) *by inspiration of God . . . "* Inspiration is composed of two Greek words meaning "God-breathed." Inspiration is the strong, conscious in-breathing of God into men, qualifying them to give utterance to Divine Truth.

Because God knew what man needs, He delivered an allied Blueprint to serve as a Producer of Pardon, Purity, and Power; thus to study the Scripture is to become aware of *"profitable . . .*

instruction, that the man of God may be perfect, thoroughly furnished unto all good works" (II Timothy 3:17).

The remaining nine names of those who labored on the **OLD GATE** unfold a superstructure of splendor erected upon the Foundation of God's Delivered, Allied Word.

It will be noted that Melatiah had a co-laborer, *"Jadon,"* whose name means, "thankful." To become spiritually aware of the enormous significance in the Wisdom of God, as expressed in His Written Word, is calculated to draw from the inner man a harmonious anthem of thankfulness.

For an individual to practice Bible Study is to enter into a realm of praise that can only be derived from such a walk. Jeremiah, the Old Testament prophet, who wept for his people, drew comfort from God when he discovered the thrill of the **OLD GATE**. Hear him as he says: *"Thy words were found, and I did eat them; and Thy word was unto me the joy and rejoicing of mine heart: for I am called by Thy name, O Lord God of hosts"* (Jeremiah 15:16). When all around was dark with despair, Jeremiah maintained a thankful attitude through the Holy Scriptures.

In Acts 17:11, Paul commended the church at Berea by stating: *"These were more noble than those in Thessalonica, in that they received the word with all readiness of mind, and searched the scriptures daily, whether those things were so."*

Bible Study will dispel the whining and melt the language of ungrateful mumbling. The **OLD GATE** will allow the Christian to not only see, but also to understand and partake in the beauty of Colossians 3:15-17 – *"And let the peace of God rule in your hearts, to the which also ye are called in one body; and be ye thankful. Let the word of Christ dwell in you richly in all wisdom; teaching and admonishing one another in psalms and hymns and spiritual songs, singing with grace in your hearts to the Lord. And whatsoever ye do in word or deed, do all in the name of the Lord Jesus, giving thanks to God and the Father by Him."*

"And next unto him repaired Uzziel," which means, "the strength of God." To study the Bible is to discover that the Christian need not

stand in his or her own power, but rather has a Source of Strength which surpasses any and all of a man-made nature; Hebrews 4:12, tells us that *"the Word of God is . . . powerful."*

The believer who stands in and by the Strength of the Bible, not petty theories or vain conjectures, moves steadily out of the realm of weak, unstable attitudes and enters the realm of strong, solid altitudes. The **OLD GATE** will cause the trembling knees to be still, the frail arms to bulge with spiritual muscularity, the jelly backbone to be transformed into a column of uprightness, and the fearful eyes to take on a gleam of holy boldness.

Though Satan may cast fiery darts in the direction of a Christian, the student of God's Word can resist the evil one, even as did Jesus, with words the devil cannot overcome: "*. . . man shall not live by bread alone, but by every Word that proceedeth out of the mouth of God*" (Matthew 4:4). Just as Christ overcame, so can we by the strength of the Word.

"And next unto him also repaired Hananiah," which means, "whom Jehovah favors." Some Christians spend too much of their lifetime wondering why others seem to always enjoy more of their religion than do they. The answer is very simple. Bible Study ushers an individual into God's special favor.

While it is true *"that God is no respecter of persons"* (Acts 10:34), for He has provided for one what He has provided for another; the difference is in the fact that some avail themselves of God's provisions, while others neglect them. God does not force one to study; He simply makes His Word available and then individuals decide how they will spend their Christian energies.

In Daniel 1:9, these words are found: *"Now God had brought Daniel into favor . . . "* Why? Was it because God was prejudice? Did He show respect of persons in an unjust manner? No. The answer can be found in Daniel 1:8 – *"But Daniel purposed in his heart that he would not defile himself with the portion of the king's meat, nor with the wine which he drank: therefore he requested of the prince of the eunuchs that he might not defile himself."* This young man had read, studied, and absorbed what Moses had penned in Leviticus 11, concerning clean and unclean foods, and being convinced by the Word, Daniel committed himself into the hands of God. When a person does this, what else can God do but to show favor!

How well Solomon conveyed this truth in Proverbs 16:7. *"When a man's ways please the Lord, He maketh even his enemies to be at peace with him."*

Not only was Daniel a man who prayed at least three times daily, but he was a man who studied the Scriptures. Some think Daniel just happened to be brilliant and an interpreter of dreams, but how our hearts should pound when we read such passages as Daniel 9:2 – *"In the first year of his reign I Daniel understood by books the number of the years, whereof the word of the LORD came to Jeremiah the prophet, that he would accomplish seventy years in the desolations of Jerusalem."* The **OLD GATE** allows an individual to be favored of God.

"And next unto them repaired Rephaiah," which means, "cured or healed by Jehovah." Not only does Bible Study inform us that healing is available, but God's Word and the digestion thereof will actually bring about healing, both spiritual and physical. Much could be written on this thought, so allow me to briefly bring to our attention these verses which convey the healing ability of the Bible and will serve to steer us in the direction of a deeper search into this truth.

First, Spiritual Healing. Romans 1:16,17 – *"For I am not ashamed of the gospel of Christ: for it is the power of God unto salvation to every one that believeth; to the Jew first, and also to the Greek. For therein is the righteousness of God revealed from faith to faith: as it is written, The just shall live by faith."* And so, the Word heals INITIALLY and CONTINUES to keep the believing, attentive one in a progressive fashion as the Gospel of Jesus is lived by faith.

Second, Physical Healing. Proverbs 4:20-22 – *"My son, attend to my words; incline thine ear unto my sayings. Let them not depart from thine eyes; keep them in the midst of thine heart. For they are life unto those that find them, and health to all their flesh."* Psalms

107:20 – *"He sent His word, and healed them, and delivered them from their destructions."*

"And next unto them repaired Jedaiah," which means, "praised or blessed of God." Spiritual blessings are bestowed upon Christians for at least two reasons: First, because one may need the blessing to serve as a booster to his or her faith; Second, because one deserves the blessing due to his or her faith.

God takes special delight in blessing His people and the Bible student stands under a continual fountain of Heavenly Showers. The following Scripture passage can awaken our awareness to what we're missing if we are not **OLD GATE** adherents. *"Blessed is the man that walketh not in the counsel of the ungodly, nor standeth in the way of sinners, nor sitteth in the seat of the scornful. But his delight is in the law of the Lord; and in His law doth he meditate day and night. And he shall be like a tree planted by the rivers of water, that bringeth forth his fruit in his season; his leaf also shall not wither; and whatsoever he doeth shall prosper"* (Psalms 1:1-3).

Can you not sense the balanced beauty of this type of Christian in comparison to the one who neglects to feast on God's Word? The Scriptures are a deep, clear running river and supply all the moisture the Christian needs to give fruit to those in need and at the same time show forth a character that is not dry and barren, but rather is green and full; not because of self, but because God has blessed in accord with the Word.

The one who desires to walk in the benefits of the **OLD GATE** must continually give an ear to the message of Jesus as He challenges in Luke 11:28 – *"BLESSED are they that HEAR the Word of God, and KEEP it."*

Have you ever heard anyone say, "I just can't understand the Bible?" If you have, and asked that person if he or she had ever read the Bible through even once, most likely you would have received a negative reply. The reason some do not understand the Word and spend much of their time in the mire of defeat is because they do not study. God wants to bless each of His children in a special manner and the way He will do so is as we allow Him. John gives hearty advice in Revelation 1:3 – *"Blessed is he that readeth, and they that hear the words of this prophecy, and keep those things which are written therein: for the time is at hand."* Allow God to bless you – STUDY.

"And next unto him repaired Hattush," which means, "gathered together." As the body that God has tempered together, there should be no schism (I Corinthians 12:24,25), within His workmanship. The only way Satan can divide Christians is as we cease to *"be perfectly joined together in the same mind and in the same judgment"* (I Corinthians 1:10), and this can only be accomplished when we take our eye off God's Word. God's Book is not the author of confusion.

There are many kinds of fellowship available to people, but none can measure unto the one enjoyed by Christians who love the Christ of the Bible. John expressed it like this in I John 1:3-7 – *"That which we have seen and heard declare we unto you, that ye also may have fellowship with us: and truly our fellowship is with the Father, and with His Son Jesus Christ. And these things write we unto you, that your joy may be full. This then is the message which we have heard of Him, and declare unto you, that God is light, and in Him is no darkness at all. If we say that we have fellowship with Him, and walk in darkness, we lie, and do not the truth: But if we walk in the light, as He is in the light, we have fellowship one with another, and the blood of Jesus Christ His Son cleanseth us from all sin."*

To walk in the light is to live in fellowship with the Word and to live in fellowship with the Word is to have fellowship with fellow believers.

We as members of God's church need to reside in the presence of the **OLD GATE**, and experience the gathering together, the unity of purpose, which is so vital to insure victory. Bible Study will bring sincere parts of the body of Christ together into a perfect vessel, fit for the Master's use.

"Malchijah . . . repaired the other side . . ." Malchijah means "Jehovah is King." The central theme of Scripture is that God is the *"lofty One that inhabiteth eternity, Whose Name is Holy"* (Isaiah 57:15), and wants to save fallen mankind (John 3:16).

The one who spends time studying the Word of the Lord becomes convicted and convinced that *"God is True and an Everlasting King"* (Jeremiah 10:10), and is able to testify to the pauper or potentate that *"I praise and extol and honor the King of heaven, Whose works are truth, and ways justice"* (Daniel 4:37).

God wants to be supreme in the heart and hopes of every Christian and the **OLD GATE** tells us that man without God is nothing, but God without man is still God. Jesus does not want to rule over just one part of the life, but He wants to be King over every portion of the being.

To see God now, by the eye of faith, through the Communication of Holy Writ as *"my King, and my God"* (Psalms 5:2), and to keep the eye single to the glory thereof is to be assured that one day we will see Him, face to face, and behold His Immeasurable Glory, as *"Lord of lords, and King of kings"* (Revelation 17:14).

Malchijah had a co-laborer named *"Hashub,"* whose name means "intelligent." To be enlightened to the significance of God's Word and His Kingship is to enter into the realm of true intelligence. A person does not go to bed ignorant and awaken the next morning as a walking, talking Bible. There must be a sincere, continual commitment to investigate the Truth of God.

Scripture intelligence comes through study, and if one will apply himself or herself, there will be a Divine assistance which will make understanding much easier. I Corinthians 12:8 – *"For to one is given by the Spirit the word of wisdom; to another the word of knowledge by the same Spirit."* Paul reminded Timothy that, *"from a child thou hast known the Holy Scriptures, which are able to make thee WISE unto salvation through faith which is in Christ Jesus"* (II Timothy 3:15).

It does not please God for His children to always play in the shallow water and continually desire nothing more solid than mere milk. He has prepared a table of banquet measure and wise is the one who partakes thereof. The church needs, in a desperate way, those who will allow the Spirit of God to impress the value of being able to testify as did the Psalmist: *"O how love I Thy law! It is my meditation all the day. Thou through Thy commandments hast made me wiser than mine enemies: for they are ever with me. I have more understanding than all my teachers: for Thy testimonies are my meditation. I understand more than the ancients, because I keep Thy precepts. I have refrained my feet from every evil way, that I might keep Thy word. I have not departed from Thy judgments: for Thou hast taught me. How sweet are Thy words unto my taste! yea, sweeter than honey to my mouth! Through Thy precepts I get understanding: therefore I hate every false way"* (Psalms 119:97-104).

"And next unto him repaired Shallum," which means "retribution." Retribution simply means reward or punishment for deeds done in this life.

Deuteronomy 18:18,19 – *"I will raise them up a Prophet from among their brethren, like unto thee, and will put My words in His mouth; and He shall speak unto them all that I shall command Him. And it shall come to pass, that whosoever will not hearken unto My words which He shall speak in My name, I will require it of him."*

Jesus said, *"He that rejecteth Me, and receiveth not My words, hath One that judgeth him: the word that I have spoken, the same shall judge him in the last day"* (John 12:48).

John recorded for the admonition of all mankind, Revelation 20:12 – *"And I saw the dead, small and great, stand before God; and the books were opened: and another book was opened, which is the book of life: and the dead were judged out of those things which were written in the books, according to their works."*

How we respect the Bible will determine the degree of reward or condemnation which will be assigned when our name comes before the Almighty at the time of judgment.

God desires that we take advantage of the **OLD GATE**. As Paul encouraged the church at Colosse, so let us be encouraged in these last days: *"Let the Word of Christ dwell in you richly . . . "* (Colossians 3:16). And this can be a reality as we heed the beckoning plea of Proverbs 4:13 – *"Take fast hold of instruction; let her not go: keep her; for she is thy life."*

Chapter Four

THE VALLEY GATE

*"The **valley gate** repaired Hanun, and the inhabitants of Zanoah; they built it, and set up the doors thereof, the locks thereof, and the bars thereof, and a thousand cubits on the wall unto the dung gate."*

(Nehemiah 3:13)

This gate Spiritually Signifies the **trials and tests which Christians face**. It is the proving ground for those who claim salvation and a desire to serve God. Most would probably agree that it is quite easy to live a Christian life while running, leaping, and skipping on the spiritual mountains, but often the tune changes when the valley becomes the way for true investigation.

There are two Greek words for "test":

1. "Dokimadzo"—for the purpose of approving. This word has in it the idea of proving a thing, whether it is worthy to receive or not, and implies that the trial was made in the expectation and hope that the end would prove victorious.
2. "Peiradzo"—to try or test intentionally with the purpose of discovering what good or evil, power or weakness is in a person or thing. This word has in it the idea of testing with a possibility of breaking down under the test.

"Dokimadzo" is never used of the testing caused by Satan. It is used generally of the trials and tests allowed by God.

Since God's Ways are far above our understanding and reasoning capabilities in regard to the fullness of the Atonement in respect to every individual, we must have faith in His Administrative Way of doing things to the Glory of His Name and the building of our Christian character.

We need to understand and accept certain principles about trials and testings.

First, trials and testings are the common lot of man. Before many seconds pass, each newborn infant becomes acquainted with the feel of pain and presence of trouble. All of mankind has inherited the curse placed on the first man because of his direct disobedience to God, and just because we become a Christian does not remove us from the presence of the **VALLEY GATE**. Walking through the **SHEEP GATE** does not promise to rid us from afflictions, but the Christ of the Cross, the Great Shepherd, does promise to give us grace sufficient to live a victorious testimony – whether on the mountain or in the valley – whether in health or in sickness.

It was Job, a man of personal experience with the agony of afflictions, who echoed, *"Man that is born of a woman is of few days and full of trouble"* (Job 14:1).

Second, trials and testings are sometimes allowed by God as a way of correcting us when we stray from His will. This has been the pattern since man's fall from Pure Communion with his Creator. As the intensity of sin did occasion, so did the correction measure become intensified.

David seemed to reflect over the Egyptian captivity and the multiple of times Israel did that which was right in their own eyes during the time of the judges. Almost tearfully we hear David as he laments and then blesses God for His gracious benefits. *"Thou broughtest us into the net; Thou laidst affliction upon our loins. Thou hast caused men to ride over our heads; we went through fire and through water: but Thou broughtest us out into a wealthy place"* (Psalms 66:11,12).

Third, trials and testings are sometimes allowed by God because the valley has a refining influence. Isaiah 48:10,11 – *"Behold, I have refined thee, but not with silver; I have chosen thee in the furnace of affliction. For Mine own sake, even for Mine own sake, will I do it:*

for how should My name be polluted? and I will not give My glory unto another."

Before we can be used of God to a rewarding Glory to His Name, we must be purged from all the weights, measures, and dross which has encircled our lives for so long. Some do not enjoy meditating on this truth, but nevertheless it is a fact which cannot – must not be overlooked. True, it is not pleasant for one to think upon, but to understand and accept the **VALLEY GATE** is calculated to do us good.

All great individuals who are indeed Biblical giants first walked through the valley so as to present themselves worthy of leadership and the accompanying responsibility.

1. Abraham, when he was tried, offered up Isaac (Hebrews 11:17).
2. Moses was in the desert for 40 years to allow him time to forget the luxury and pleasures of Egypt.
3. Daniel in the lion's den.
4. Paul in the Arabian desert.

Before the steel structure can go into the supporting position of a lovely new building, it first has to be taken as a raw piece of ore and be cast into the melting pot from where it is taken and shaped into the fashion of best usefulness. Who knows what you and I would turn out to be like if God did not allow us to be afflicted so as to remind us that we are but sinners saved by His Grace and Love.

Many times the Christian is indeed matured by valleys, trials, and testings. The New Testament writer Paul was well qualified to speak on this subject. *"And not only so, but we glory in tribulations also: knowing that tribulation worketh patience; And patience, experience; and experience, hope: And hope maketh not ashamed; because the love of God is shed abroad in our hearts by the Holy Ghost which is given unto us"* (Romans 5:3-5).

James, the practical apostle, also addressed this issue – *"My brethren, count it all joy when ye fall into divers temptations; Knowing this, that the trying of your faith worketh patience"* (James 1:2,3).

There were two personalities who labored on the **VALLEY GATE**: *"Hanun"* and *"the inhabitants of Zanoah."*

Hanun means "whom God pities." The Christian who is enduring trials must never, for one moment, entertain the thought that God has forsaken him or her.

In the Scriptures, David is acknowledged for being *"a man after God's own heart"* (I Samuel 13:14; Acts 13:22). Why? Because he could say, *"Yea, though I walk through the **VALLEY** . . . I will fear no evil: for Thou art with me; Thy rod and Thy staff they comfort me"* (Psalms 23:4).

Later, Paul would write these words to the church at Corinth, which was traveling through some rough times: *"Blessed be God, even the Father of our Lord Jesus Christ, the Father of mercies, and the God of all comfort; Who comforteth us in all our tribulation, that we may be able to comfort them which are in any trouble, by the comfort wherewith we ourselves are comforted of God. For as the sufferings of Christ abound in us, so our consolation also aboundeth by Christ. And whether we be afflicted, it is for your consolation and salvation, which is effectual in the enduring of the same sufferings which we also suffer: or whether we be comforted, it is for your consolation and salvation. And our hope of you is stedfast, knowing, that as ye are partakers of the sufferings, so shall ye be also of the consolation"* (II Corinthians 1:3-7).

There are seven crowns mentioned in the Bible and James mentions one in relation with those who endure trials. *"Blessed is the man that endureth temptation: for when he is tried, he shall receive the crown of life, which the Lord hath promised to them that love Him"* (James 1:12).

Some trials or tests may be brief, but we must not despair if others seem lengthy. Nehemiah 3:13, speaks of a *"1000 cubits,"* which equals approximately 1800 feet – quite a length indeed.

The Bible informs us that Israel had to defeat 31 kings across the Jordan River when they finally arrived in the Promised Land. That equals one king for each day of the longest month.

What we must accept by faith is that even though the trial may be lengthy, God has made a provision for victory. *"There hath no temptation taken you but such as is common to man: but God is faithful, Who will not suffer you to be tempted above that ye are able; but will with the temptation also make a way to escape, that ye may be able to bear it"* (I Corinthians 10:13).

"The inhabitants of Zanoah" also worked on the **VALLEY GATE**. Zanoah means "rejected."

We are living in a strange time. Some are preaching and teaching that all trials, testings, and afflictions are the result of a lack of faith on an individual's part. To believe some of the modern interpretations concerning valleys is enough to cause one to throw up his or her hands in despair, were it not for the **OLD GATE** which prepares us for the **VALLEY GATE**.

The believer in God does not reject the trials associated with the **VALLEY GATE**, but resounds with lip and life, *"we glory in tribulations"* (Romans 5:3); *"I am exceeding joyful in all our tribulation"* (II Corinthians 7:4).

The practice of studying the Scriptures helps us stand on the FACT of **OLD GATE** Bible Truth and to place our FAITH in God's ability to help us so that we will not walk by FEELINGS, but by FAITH in God's FACT.

Those who walk by FEELINGS soon grow weary when the **VALLEY GATE** is a part of the Christian journey, but those who walk by FAITH remember the words of Jesus in John 16:31-33 – *"Jesus answered them, Do ye now believe? Behold, the hour cometh, yea, is now come, that ye shall be scattered, every man to his own, and shall leave Me alone: and yet I am not alone, because the Father is with Me. These things I have spoken unto you, that in Me ye might have peace. In the world ye SHALL have tribulation: but be of good cheer; I have overcome the world."*

The early church understood this principle and our church age must have a revival of this FACT. It will do us well to not only read, but to accept Acts 14:22, with a joyful countenance. *"Confirming the souls of the disciples, and exhorting them to continue in the faith, and that WE*

MUST THROUGH MUCH TRIBULATION enter into the kingdom of God." The Christian is to Scripturally and Spiritually understand *"that all things work together for good to them that love God, to them who are the called according to His purpose"* (Romans 8:28).

Therefore, we must not allow man or Satan to lead us in rejection or rebellion against God's Word, Will, and Way; in order *"that no man should be moved by these afflictions: for yourselves know that we are appointed thereunto"* (I Thessalonians 3:3).

As Christians we must allow Christ to be our Example in all things, even in the area of the **VALLEY GATE** of trials and sufferings: *"For consider Him that endured such contradiction of sinners against Himself, lest ye be wearied and faint in your minds"* (Hebrews 12:3); *"For we have not an High Priest which cannot be touched with the feeling of our infirmities; but was in all points tempted like as we are, yet without sin"* (Hebrews 4:15).

As members of God's family we need not be dismayed, disheartened, discouraged, or defeated because of the **VALLEY GATE**. The Lord will raise the afflicted one. Soon we will lay aside this robe of flesh and know the pain of affliction no longer.

The apostle Peter is considered by many to be an authority in relation to trials, testings, and afflictions. At least fifteen times in the two epistles which bear his name, this subject is dealt with and First Peter is called "The Christian Code Of Suffering." With a soothing tone he wrote these words: *"Who are kept by the power of God through faith unto salvation ready to be revealed in the last time. Wherein ye greatly rejoice, though now for a season, if need be, ye are in heaviness through manifold temptations: That the trial of your faith, being much more precious than of gold that perisheth, though it be tried with fire, might be found unto praise and honour and glory at the appearing of Jesus Christ"* (I Peter 1:5-7).

God grant that each of us will be enabled to find assurance and comfort as His child – even at the **VALLEY GATE.**

Chapter Five

THE DUNG GATE

*"But the **dung gate** repaired Malchiah the son of Rechab, the ruler of part of Bethhaccerem; he built it, and set up the doors thereof, the locks thereof, and the bars thereof."*

(Nehemiah 3:14)

Geographically, the **DUNG GATE** led to the waste disposal area outside the city. The Spiritual Significance of this gate is that it **represents the getting rid of excesses in our lives.** Dung is the waste which tends to stagnate one's life and mar the environmental surroundings.

Satan is ever busy endeavoring to get us to take on more of the world and its things. Several years ago I came across this poem. Since the author is unknown, credit for its origin cannot be given.

The Church Walking With The World

The Church and the world walked far apart, On the changing shores of time;
The world was singing a giddy song, And the Church a hymn sublime.
"Come, give me your hand," said the merry world, "And walk with me this way!"
But the good Church hid her snowy hands, And solemnly answered "Nay;
I will not give you my hand at all, And I will not walk with you;
Your way is the way that leads to death; Your words are all untrue."

"Nay, walk with me but a little space," Said the world with a kindly air;
"The road I walk is a pleasant road, And the sunshine always there;
Your path is thorny and rough and rude, But mine is broad and plain;
My way is paved with flowers and dews, And yours with tears and pain;

The sky to me is always blue, No want, no toil I know;
The sky above you is always dark, Your lot is a lot of woe;
There's room enough for you and me, To travel side by side."

Half shyly the Church approached the world, And gave him her hand of snow;
And the world grasped it and walked along, Saying, in accents low,
"Your dress is too simple to please my taste, I will give you pearls to wear,
Rich velvets and silks for your graceful form, And diamonds to deck your hair."
The Church looked down at her plain white robes, And then at the dazzling world,
And blushed as she saw his handsome lip, With a smile contemptuous curled.
"I will change my dress for a costlier one," Said the Church, with a smile of grace;
Then her pure white garments drifted away, And the world gave, in their place,
Beautiful satins and shining silks, Roses and gems and costly pearls;
While over her forehead her bright hair fell, Crisped in a thousand curls.

"Your house is too plain," said the proud old world, "I'll build you one like mine;
With walls of marble and towers of gold, And furniture ever so fine."
So he built her a costly and beautiful house; Most splendid it was to behold;
Her sons and her beautiful daughters dwelt there, Gleaming in purple and gold;
Rich fairs and shows in the halls were held, And the world and his children were there.
Laughter and music and feasts were heard, In the place that was meant for prayer;
There were cushioned seats for the rich of that day, To sit in their pomp and pride;
But the poor who were clad in shabby array, Sat meekly down outside.

"You give too much to the poor," said the world, "Far more than you ought to do;
If they are in need of shelter and food, Why need it trouble you?
Go, take your money and buy rich robes, Buy houses, land, and cars that are fine;
Buy pearls and jewels and dainty food, Buy the rarest and costliest wine;
My children, they dote on all these things, And if you their love would win
You must do as they do, and walk in the ways, That they are walking in."
So the poor were turned from her door in scorn, And she heard not the orphan's cry;
But she drew her beautiful robes aside, As the widows went weeping by.

Then the sons of the world and the sons of the Church, Walked closely hand and heart;
And only the Master, Who knoweth all, Could tell the two apart.
Then the Church sat down at her ease and said, "I am rich and my goods increase;
I have need of nothing, or aught to do, But to laugh and dance and feast."

The sly world heard, and he laughed in his sleeve, And mockingly said, aside –
"The Church is fallen, the beautiful Church; And her shame is her boast and her pride."

The angels drew near to the Mercy Seat, And whispered in sighs her name;
Then the loud anthems of rapture were hushed, And heads were covered with shame;
And a Voice was heard at last by the Church, From Him Who sat on the throne,
"I know thy works, and how thou hast said, I am rich, and hast not known
That thou art naked, poor, and blind, And wretched before My face;
Therefore from My presence cast thee out, And blot thy name from its place."

Jesus gave a solemn warning to the Church Age which would be present just prior to His Second Return, and you and I are a part of this even today. It is referred to as the Church Of Laodicea. Without sounding preachy or judgmental, the sincere observer of contemporary action and interaction has to agree, at least to some degree, that it is becoming more and more difficult to distinguish between the church and the world. Our speech, our eating and drinking habits, our clothing, our choices for entertainment – all tend to be an area of confusion to someone who is searching for a different lifestyle than that which the world practices and offers.

To accept the Spiritual and Scriptural Significance of the **DUNG GATE** enforces our desire to heed the commandment given by our Loving Heavenly Father, found in I John 2:15, 16. *"Love not the world, neither the things that are in the world. If any man love the world, the love of the Father is not in him. For all that is in the world, the lust of the flesh, and the lust of the eyes, and the pride of life, is not of the Father, but is of the world."*

Just as excess physical weight is a hindrance, even so excess cargo relative to our relationship with the world is a spiritual hindrance. No wonder the apostle was inspired to write this message in Hebrews 12:1 – *"Wherefore seeing we also are compassed about with so great a cloud of witnesses, let us lay aside every weight, and the sin which doth so easily beset us, and let us run with patience the race that is set before us."*

That the **DUNG GATE** follows the **VALLEY GATE** is no coincidence. As we understand and accept the principles associated with **VALLEY GATE** trials and testings, and continue our pilgrimage through the **DUNG GATE**, we become greatly enlightened to the realization that we are nothing of meaningful importance except by the Grace of our Risen Saviour.

This reality is expressed so beautifully in the meaning of the name of the personality involved in the work on this gate. *"Malchiah"* means "Jehovah Is King."

If a follower of Jesus is ever to fulfill God's Perfect Will, he or she must come to the place where the testimony of John the Baptist flows from one's life and lips: *"He* (Christ) *must increase, but I must decrease"* (John 3:30).

To understand the **DUNG GATE** importance in our Christian journey is to realize the value of what Paul expressed in II Corinthians 4:7 – *"But we have this treasure in earthen vessels, that the excellency of the power may be of God, and not of us."* God must be our Leader – Jesus must be our King.

Self denial is not a virtue of natural man, but self denial is still the invitation of Jesus to each one who would be His disciple. It will do us well to not only hear, but also heed this compassionate invitation because as Christ continued to explain in question form, our choice is of eternal significance: *"Then said Jesus unto His disciples, If any man will come after Me, let him deny himself, and take up his cross, and follow Me. For whosoever will save his life shall lose it: and whosoever will lose his life for My sake shall find it. For what is a man profited, if he shall gain the whole world, and lose his own soul? or what shall a man give in exchange for his soul?"* (Matthew 16:24-26).

Whether Malchiah or his father was *"the ruler of part of Bethhaccerem"* is not clear from Nehemiah 3:14. However, the meaning of *"Bethhaccerem"* is intriguing. It means "house or place of the vineyard."

When one realizes and appropriates this truth, the **DUNG GATE** then begins to re-fertilize the individual's life and he or she is ushered into the splendor of John 15:1-5 – *"I am the True Vine, and*

My Father is the Husbandman. Every branch in Me that beareth not fruit He taketh away: and every branch that beareth fruit, He purgeth it, that it may bring forth more fruit. Now ye are clean through the Word which I have spoken unto you. Abide in Me, and I in you. As the branch cannot bear fruit of itself, except it abide in the vine; no more can ye, except ye abide in Me. I am the Vine. Ye are the branches: He that abideth in Me, and Me in him, the same bringeth forth much fruit: for without Me ye can do nothing."

Paul certainly came to understand what Jesus meant, because his personal testimony exudes as much more than just a philosophy, it was his lifestyle – not just his way of living:

I Corinthians 6:12 – *"All things are lawful unto me, but all things are not expedient: all things are lawful for me, but I will not be brought under the power of any."*

I Corinthians 10:23 – *"All things are lawful for me, but all things are not expedient: all things are lawful for me, but all things edify not."*

Philippians 3:8 – *"Yea, doubtless, and I count all things but loss for the excellency of the knowledge of Christ Jesus my Lord: for Whom I have suffered the loss of all things, and do count them but* ***DUNG****, that I may win Christ."*

Isn't it interesting that Paul used this very word, **DUNG**, to convey the concept of God relative to the issue of not becoming entangled with things which violate His Word, Will, and Way? Coincidence? No! It is another evidence of the Continuing Miracle Of Divine Revelation.

Indeed, the Scriptures teach that the way to obtain favor with God is to exhibit the spirit of the **DUNG GATE**. Saul, the first king of Israel is a prime example. I Samuel 15:17 – *"And Samuel said*(to Saul), *When thou wast little in thine own sight, wast thou not made the head of the tribes of Israel, and the Lord anointed thee king over Israel?"* However, as wonderful as this statement is, our hearts are saddened when we are confronted with how Saul's reign ended – and the tragedy unfolded due to his failure to continue in the spirit of the **DUNG GATE**.

Refusal to the process of putting away excesses will clog us with unnecessary attitudes which cause the existence of our lives to forfeit the manifold blessing of a Saviour Who longs to enable us to be productive. But, on the other hand, the putting away of excesses will lead to our lives becoming as a vineyard filled with good fruit.

The **DUNG GATE** involves a twofold process. It involves both **putting on** and **putting off**. This Scriptural, Spiritual Concept is expressed with great clarity in Ephesians 4.

First, the putting on (verses 23,24,32). *"And be renewed in the spirit of your mind; And that ye put on the new man, which after God is created in righteousness and true holiness . . . And be ye kind one to another, tenderhearted, forgiving one another, even as God for Christ's sake hath forgiven you."*

Second, the putting off (verses 17-22, 25-31). *"This I say therefore, and testify in the Lord, that ye henceforth walk not as other Gentiles walk, in the vanity of their mind, Having the understanding darkened, being alienated from the life of God through the ignorance that is in them, because of the blindness of their heart: Who being past feeling have given themselves over unto lasciviousness, to work all uncleanness with greediness. But ye have not so learned Christ; If so be that ye have heard Him, and have been taught by Him, as the truth is in Jesus: That ye put off concerning the former conversation the old man, which is corrupt according to the deceitful lusts; Wherefore putting away lying, speak every man truth with his neighbour: for we are members one of another. Be ye angry, and sin not: let not the sun go down upon your wrath: Neither give place to the devil. Let him that stole steal no more: but rather let him labour, working with his hands the thing which is good, that he may have to give to him that needeth. Let no corrupt communication proceed out of your mouth, but that which is good to the use of edifying, that it may minister grace unto the hearers. And grieve not the holy Spirit of God, whereby ye are sealed unto the day of redemption. Let all bitterness, and wrath, and anger, and clamour, and evil speaking, be put away from you, with all malice."*

The Christian who is a diligent student at the **OLD GATE** becomes both convicted and convinced that God has placed the **DUNG GATE** to be a vital part of our relationship with Him and the world, not to hurt us, but to help us – not to keep us from enjoying life, but rather to assist us in rejoicing in a more abundant life. Anything we lay aside for the cause of our Spiritual Progress will not be missed, because the provisions of the Lord which we take on are so much more splendorous.

Chapter Six

THE FOUNTAIN GATE

"But the gate of the fountain repaired Shallun the son of Colhozeh, the ruler of part of Mizpah; he built it, and covered it, and set up the doors thereof, the locks thereof, and the bars thereof, and the wall of the pool of Hiloah by the king's garden, and unto the stairs that go down from the city of David. After him repaired Nehemiah the son of Azbuk, the ruler of the half part of Bethzur, unto the place over against the sepulchres of David, and to the pool that was made, and unto the house of the mighty. After him repaired the Levites, Rehum the son of Bani. Next unto him repaired Hashabiah, the ruler of the half part of Keilah, in his part. After him repaired their brethren, Bavai the son of Henadad, the ruler of the half part of Keilah. And next to him repaired Ezer the son of Jeshua, the ruler of Mizpah, another piece over against the going up to the armoury at the turning of the wall. After him Baruch the son of Zabbai earnestly repaired the other piece, from the turning of the wall unto the door of the house of Eliashib the high priest. After him repaired Meremoth the son of Urijah the son of Koz another piece, from the door of the house of Eliashib eve to the end of the house of Eliashib. After him repaired the priests, the men of the plain. After him repaired Benjamin and Hashub over against their house. After him repaired Azariah the son of Maaseiah the son of Ananiah by his house. After him repaired Binnui the son of Henadad another piece, from the house of Azariah unto the turning of the wall, even unto the corner. Palal the son of

Uzai, over against the turning of the wall, and the tower which lieth out of the king's high house, that was by the court of the prison. After him Pedaiah the son of Parosh."
(Nehemiah 3:15-25)

The **FOUNTAIN GATE** Spiritually Signifies the **process of Sanctification in a person's life and the praise we can give to God for the victory He enables us to experience.** When one comes to the place of humility and willingness to totally lean on the everlasting arms of Christ, rather than the weak limbs of the world, then he or she is ready for a fountain to be opened whereby the character can take on more and more of the likeness of our Perfect Example, Jesus Christ. Ephesians 4:13 – *"Till we all come in the unity of the faith, and the knowledge of the Son of God, unto a perfect man, unto the measure of the stature of the fulness of Christ."*

Zechariah knew something of the power of this fountain as clearly expressed in these words: *"In that day there shall be a fountain opened to the house of David and to the inhabitants of Jerusalem for sin and for uncleanness"* (Zechariah 13:1).

As we allow the **OLD GATE** of Bible Study to reveal the Character of Christ, which God longs to reproduce in us; as we walk through the **VALLEY GATE** of Trials so as to learn that indeed *"all things work together for good to them that love God"* (Romans 8:28); as we walk through the **DUNG GATE** and come to understand that even after becoming a child of God there are excesses in our lives which must be surrendered so as not to stagnate our journey, the significance of the **FOUNTAIN GATE** intensifies.

The **SHEEP GATE**, that we looked at initially, brings us into relationship with God as Father and child because we confess our sins and accept His forgiveness, but the **FOUNTAIN GATE** assures us that not only can our sins be forgiven, but also of the truth that as we surrender to Christ and commit our way to Him, He is able to give us victory over the evil one and the *"sin which doth so easily beset us"* (Hebrews 12:1).

We might say that God desires us to be free from sin and sinning. The words of the hymn "Rock Of Ages" describe this concept:

"Rock of Ages, cleft for me, Let me hide myself in Thee;
Let the water and the blood, From Thy riven side which flowed,
Be of sin the double cure, Cleanse me from its guilt and power."

If there were no **FOUNTAIN GATE**, the guilt which can be produced by the **DUNG GATE** would be overwhelming. Each of us, as children of God, have our unique struggles and battles as expressed in Romans 7. *"For we know that the law is spiritual: but I am carnal, sold under sin. For that which I do I allow not: for what I would, that do I not; but what I hate, that do I. If then I do that which I would not, I consent unto the law that it is good. Now then it is no more I that do it, but sin that dwelleth in me. For I know that in me (that is, in my flesh,) dwelleth no good thing: for to will is present with me; but how to perform that which is good I find not. For the good that I would I do not: but the evil which I would not, that I do. Now if I do that I would not, it is no more I that do it, but sin that dwelleth in me. I find then a law, that, when I would do good, evil is present with me. For I delight in the law of God after the inward man: But I see another law in my members, warring against the law of my mind, and bringing me into captivity to the law of sin which is in my members. O wretched man that I am! who shall deliver me from the body of this death? I thank God through Jesus Christ our Lord. So then with the mind I myself serve the law of God; but with the flesh the law of sin"* (Romans 7:14-25).

The enemy of our soul delights to constantly allude to this war so as to cause us to feel guilt and condemnation. But we can be thankful for the **FOUNTAIN GATE** and the liberating assurance of Romans 8:1-4 – *"There is therefore now no condemnation to them which are in Christ Jesus, who walk not after the flesh, but after the Spirit. For the law of the Spirit of life in Christ Jesus hath made me free from the law of sin and death. For what the law could not do, in that it was weak through the flesh, God sending His own Son in the likeness of* *sinful flesh, and for sin, condemned sin in the flesh: That the righteousness of the law might be fulfilled in us, who walk not after the flesh, but after the Spirit."*

How did Jesus condemn sin in the flesh? Hebrews 13:12, gives us the answer. *"Wherefore Jesus also, that He might sanctify the people with His own blood,* ***suffered without the gate.****"*

It is one thing to know intellectually that Jesus prayed for our sanctification, but it is quite another to allow the process to flow experimentally. The invitation of Hebrews 13:13 is still a valid practice today: *"Let us go forth therefore unto Him without the camp, bearing His reproach."*

God does not want our testimonies to be lived in an uncertain manner. He has made the way for us to choose the way which is right and to be empowered to project that way unto others. James asked a rhetorical question in James 3:11. *"Doth a fountain send forth at the same place sweet water and bitter?"* Of course we agree with the answer given to that question in the very next verse and resound loud and long – an emphatic NO! *". . . no fountain can both yield salt water and fresh"* (verse 12).

To comprehend this with intellect and apprehend this with emotion is calculated to bring forth the praise mentioned in Hebrews 13:15 – *"By Him* (Jesus) *therefore let us offer the sacrifice of praise to God continually, that is, the fruit of our lips giving thanks to His name."* Remember Paul's attitude after asking who would be able to deliver him? *"I thank God through Jesus Christ our Lord . . . "* (Romans 7:25).

Satan is ever devising traps in an attempt to ensnare and defeat, but God has provided the avenue through which we can be delivered – ***"The law of the wise is a fountain of life, to depart from the snares of death"*** (Proverbs 13:14).

What is *"the law of the wise"* man? The Word of God. Oh that we could only accept the liberating quality of God's Word. Jesus prayed that we experience it in John 17:17. *"Sanctify them through Thy truth: Thy word is truth."* Earlier Jesus has explained in grand detail the freeing quality of truth. *"And ye shall know the truth, and the truth shall make you free. They answered Him, We be Abraham's seed, and were never in bondage to any man: how sayest Thou, Ye shall be made free? Jesus answered them, Verily, verily, I say unto you, Whosoever committeth sin is the servant of sin. And the servant abideth not in the house for ever: but the Son abideth ever. If the Son therefore shall make you free, ye shall be free indeed . . . he that is of God heareth God's words"* (John 8:32-36,47a).

Jesus desired for His Church to be free from sin, sinning, and the guilt thereof so much that He died to secure this possibility. Ephesians 5:25-27 – *"Husbands, love your wives, even as Christ also loved the church, and gave Himself for it; That He might sanctify and cleanse it with the washing of water by the word, That He might present it to Himself a glorious church, not having spot, or wrinkle, or any such thing; but that it should be holy and without blemish."*

God allowed His Son to die for us so that, by faith in Jesus, we might become a holy, dedicated, committed, liberated people. Paul was inspired to deal with this matter with great tenderness in the following passages:

I Thessalonians 3:9-13. *"For what thanks can we render to God again for you, for all the joy wherewith we joy for your sakes before our God; Night and day praying exceedingly that we might see your face, and might perfect that which is lacking in your faith? Now God Himself and our Father, and our Lord Jesus Christ, direct our way unto you. And the Lord make you to increase and abound in love one toward another, and toward all men, even as we do toward you: To the end He may stablish your hearts unblameable in holiness before God, even our Father, at the coming of our Lord Jesus Christ with all His saints."*

I Thessalonians 4:1-4. *"Furthermore then we beseech you, brethren, and exhort you by the Lord Jesus, that as ye have received of us how ye ought to walk and to please God, so ye would abound more and more. For ye know what commandments we gave you by the Lord Jesus. For this is the will of God, even your sanctification, that ye should abstain from fornication: That every one of you should know how to possess his vessel in sanctification and honour."*

As the song writer penned:

"There is a fountain filled with blood, Drawn from Immanuel's veins;
And sinners plunged beneath that flood, Lose all their guilty stains,
The dying thief rejoiced to see, That fountain in his day;
And there may I, though vile as he, Wash all my sins away.
Thou dying Lamb! Thy precious blood, Shall never lose its power,
Till all the ransomed church of God, Are saved to sin no more."

The names of the various personalities who labored on the **FOUNTAIN GATE** reveal an uplifting portrait of the process of sanctification which is the work of a lifetime.

"Shallum" (Nehemiah 3:15) means "requittal," or "to free from unnecessary fears." How precious this fact is to the Christian.

Because we begin our journey with Jesus as spiritual infants, there will come times when we make mistakes, stumble and fall. The natural reaction on our part is to fear that because we have failed God there is no or little hope, but God says differently. He states through John, *"My little children, these things write I unto you, that ye sin not. And if any man sin, we have an Advocate with the Father, Jesus Christ the Righteous"* (I John 2:1).

The experience of Peter is a prime illustration. Peter, the fisherman who walked with Jesus for some three years; Peter, the disciple who saw the dead raised and the glory of the Christ upon the mount of transfiguration; Peter, the zealous reed shaken in the wind who boasted he would never forsake the Master, denied Jesus three times on the night of betrayal. His sin was great and yet when Jesus arose from the tomb, He sent special words of encouragement to Peter and the apostle was released from the guilt he had carried for days.

We can continually thank God for the process of sanctification which enables us, *"as newborn babes"* to *"desire the sincere milk of the word,"* that we *"may grow thereby"* (I Peter 2:2); *"grow in grace, and in the knowledge of our Lord and Saviour Jesus Christ"* (II Peter 3:18).

Nehemiah 3:15, lists three places involved with the **FOUNTAIN GATE**: 1. *"the pool of Siloah"*; 2. *"the king's garden"*; 3. *"the stairs that go down from the city of David."*

As the Christian begins to practice the lessons of the **VALLEY GATE** and the **DUNG GATE** – as trials are accepted and excesses are discarded, the life takes on more and more of the beauty of God's desire. Our life will not be stagnant, but will flow like a stream; our countenance will not be gloomy, but will exhibit the colors, fragrances, and fruit of a well-nurtured garden; our walk will not be bogged in a rut, but will ascend and descend with the attitude of the city of peace being paramount in our actions and reactions.

There is nothing depressing about the life which seeks to be committed to God's Will. This is why Paul made the following urgent appeal to the church in Romans 12:1,2 – *"I beseech you therefore, brethren, by the mercies of God, that ye present your bodies a living sacrifice, holy, acceptable unto God, which is your reasonable service. And be not conformed to this world: but be ye transformed by the renewing of your mind, that ye may prove what is that good, and acceptable, and perfect, will of God."*

The most miserable people in the church are those who know what they should be doing and kick against it. People of this makeup never seem to be quite comfortable in their fellowship with God and fellow church members, because there is a lack of surrender.

This is why the meaning of the next personality is so important. *"Nehemiah"* (Nehemiah 3:16), means "consolation" or "comfort."

Oh, that we could completely grasp the principle taught so plainly in Philippians 2. Paul begins with: *"If there be therefore any consolation in Christ, if any comfort of love, if any fellowship of the Spirit, if any bowels and mercies"* (verse 1). He then lists several concepts and deals with them. Then he arrives at the key, as recorded in verses 10 and 11 – *"That at the name of Jesus every knee should bow, of things in heaven, and things in earth, and things under the earth; And that every tongue should confess that Jesus Christ is Lord, to the glory of God the Father."*

The process of sanctification is daily being crucified with Christ; it is moment by moment surrendering to the Lordship of Jesus; it is removing hands off the Potter's wheel and saying, "My desire shall be to do Your pleasure."

God has not only called us, He has chosen us to be different from the world, and the sooner the Christian begins to abound in this, the happier he or she will be. *"But we are bound to give thanks alway to God for you, brethren beloved of the Lord, because God hath from the beginning chosen you to salvation through sanctification of the Spirit and belief of the truth: Whereunto He called you by our gospel, to the obtaining of the glory of our Lord Jesus Christ. Therefore, brethren, stand fast, and hold the traditions which ye have been taught, whether by word, or our epistle. Now our Lord Jesus Christ Himself, and God, even our Father, Which hath loved us, and hath given us everlasting consolation and good hope through grace, Comfort your hearts, and stablish you in every good word and work"* (II Thessalonians 2:13-17).

Nehemiah 3:17, mentions two personalities relative to the Levites who labored on the **FOUNTAIN GATE**: *"Rehum,"* which means "compassionate, " and *"Hashabiah,"* which means "to permeate," "to weave."

The tribe of Levi, because of their stand for God in the wilderness, was entrusted with the privilege to care for the Tabernacle and later the Temple. It was from the tribe of Levi that the priesthood emerged. Let's listen intently to our Great High Priest, as He talked to His Father concerning our sanctification, as recorded in John 17. *" Sanctify them through Thy truth: Thy word is truth . . . That they all may be one; as Thou, Father, art in Me, and I in Thee, that they also may be one in Us: that the world may believe that Thou hast sent Me. And the glory which Thou gavest Me I have given them; that they may be one, even as We are one: I in them, and Thou in Me, that they may be made perfect in one; and that the world may know that Thou hast sent Me, and hast loved them, as Thou hast loved Me.*

Father, I will that they also, whom Thou hast given Me, be with Me where I am; that they may behold My glory, which Thou hast given Me: for Thou lovedst Me before the foundation of the world. O righteous Father, the world hath not known Thee: but I have known Thee, and these have known that Thou hast sent Me. And I have declared unto them Thy name, and will declare it: that the love wherewith Thou hast loved Me may be in them, and I in them" (17,21-26).

Jesus desires that we be permeated with the Love of God, and this Love will enable us to be woven together as one body for the Glory of our Father's Name. In fact, Levi literally means, "attached." This is our potential through sanctification – To be attached to God and attached to one another.

The two personalities mentioned in Nehemiah 3:18,24, *"Bavai"* and *"Binnui,"* mean "built up." And this is God's desire for us. It is expressed by these words in Ephesians 2:19-22. *"Now therefore ye are no more strangers and foreigners, but fellowcitizens with the saints, and of the household of God; And are built upon the foundation of the apostles and prophets, Jesus Christ Himself being the Chief Corner Stone; In Whom all the building fitly framed together groweth unto an holy temple in the Lord: In Whom ye also are builded together for an habitation of God through the Spirit."*

But this kind of existence is impossible in our own strength. Through the centuries man has tried, but all one has to do is read of the atrocities of war to realize that our efforts have been futile.

It is not mere chance that linked with these two personalities, whose names mean "built up," are two personalities, *"Ezer"* (Nehemiah 3:19), and *"Azariah"* (Nehemiah 3:23), whose names also mean the same thing. Ezer means "aid or help," and Azariah means "God has helped."

"But God, Who is rich in mercy, for His great love wherewith He loved us, Even when we were dead in sins, hath quickened us together with Christ, (by grace ye are saved;) And hath raised us up together, and made us sit together in heavenly places in Christ Jesus:

That in the ages to come He might shew the exceeding riches of His grace in His kindness toward us through Christ Jesus. For by grace are ye saved through faith; and that not of yourselves: it is the gift of God: Not of works, lest any man should boast. For we are His workmanship, created in Christ Jesus unto good works, which God hath before ordained that we should walk in them" (Ephesians 2:4-10). And just in case someone might become confused as to our need for Divine Aid, listen to the information given on this subject in Philippians 2:12,13 – *"Wherefore, my beloved, as ye have always obeyed, not as in my presence only, but now much more in my absence, work out your own salvation with fear and trembling. For it is God Which worketh in you both to will and to do of His good pleasure."*

As I was studying this **FOUNTAIN GATE**, I wondered why God would emphasis this point on two occasions, and then I remembered that sanctification is not a one-time experience, but rather, sanctification is indeed the work of a lifetime. Throughout our journey God wants us to understand our desperate need for His assistance.

Why does God repeatedly appeal for us to allow Him to help? So that we might experience the exhilaration of Philippians 2:15, while we walk in the world, but remain separated from the world: *"That ye may be blameless and harmless, the sons of God, without rebuke, in the midst of a crooked and perverse nation, among whom ye shine as lights in the world."*

From this verse, two principles emerge: 1. God longs to bless His children, and 2. God longs to elevate His children.

This is exactly what is presented in the next two personalities found in Nehemiah 3:19,20. *"Baruch"* means "blessed" and *"Meremoth"* means "heights."

The Bible did not just happen to be written the way it was. Both text and context are inspired. Before noticing this truth in Matthew 5, let's reemphasize a principle: WE ARE SANCTIFIED BY THE WORD OF GOD.

In the opening verses of Matthew 5, two areas of concern flow from the heart and mouth of Jesus: First, His desire to "BLESS" (verses 3-12). Second, His desire for those who are blessed to share a testimony that will inspire others to seek this "HIGH" kind of life (verses 13-16).

Now notice how Jesus links this "BLESSED" and "HIGH" life with a separated lifestyle that is based on God's Word: *"Think not that I am come to destroy the law, or the prophets: I am not come to destroy, but to fulfil. For verily I say unto you, Till heaven and earth pass, one jot or one tittle shall in no wise pass from the law, till all be fulfilled. Whosoever therefore shall break one of these least commandments, and shall teach men so, he shall be called the least in the kingdom of heaven: but whosoever shall do and teach them, the same shall be called great in the kingdom of heaven. For I say unto you, That except your righteousness shall exceed the righteousness of the scribes and Pharisees, ye shall in no case enter into the kingdom of heaven"* (Matthew 5:17-20).

At this juncture, another very important issue surfaces: While it is true that God does the sanctifying, by His Word, God has chosen to use mankind as His appointed vessels through whom to work. Nehemiah 3:22, unveils a crucial personality. *"And after him repaired the priests, the men of the plain."*

Paul, through Spiritual Inspiration would write, hundreds of years later – *"And He* (God) *gave some, apostles; and some, prophets; and some, evangelists; and some, pastors and teachers; For the perfecting of the saints, for the work of the ministry, for the edifying of the body of Christ: Till we all come in the unity of the faith, and of the knowledge of the Son of God, unto a perfect man, unto the measure of the stature of the fulness of Christ: That we henceforth be no more children, tossed to and fro, and carried about with every wind of doctrine, by the sleight of men, and cunning craftiness, whereby they lie in wait to deceive"* (Ephesians 4:11-14).

God has instituted certain ministries in the body of Christ so that we henceforth be no more children of this world, but children of God. In Nehemiah 3:23, we discover the next two personalities depict this most vividly: *"Benjamin,"* whose name means "son of the right hand," and *"Hashub,"* whose name means "intelligent."

The Bible teaches that God allowed His Son, Jesus Christ to die, so that as we place our faith in His birth, life, death and resurrection, we can become sons and daughters of God. Look at Ephesians 5:1: *"Be ye therefore followers of God, as dear children."*

Also, the Bible teaches that we are not destined to live life in a guessing mode. We can study God's sanctifying Word, and through the Power Of His Holy Spirit make an "intelligent" decision to follow God's Word as a cherished child.

We become a child of God by coming to *"the knowledge of the Son of God"* (Ephesians 4:13); and after we become a member of His family, we must continue to make intelligent decisions – we must continue to learn of His Will for our life and living. *"This I say therefore, and testify in the Lord, that ye henceforth walk not as other Gentiles walk, in the vanity of their mind, Having the understanding darkened, being alienated from the life of God through the ignorance that is in them, because of the blindness of their heart: Who being past feeling have given themselves over unto lasciviousness, to work all uncleanness with greediness. But ye have not so learned Christ; If so be that ye have heard Him, and have been taught by Him, as the truth is in Jesus: That ye put off concerning the former conversation the old man, which is corrupt according to the deceitful lusts; And be renewed in the spirit of your mind; And that ye put on the new man, which after God is created in righteousness and true holiness"* (Ephesians 4:17-24).

"RIGHTEOUSNESS AND TRUE HOLINESS" – SANCTIFICATION – GOD'S PROVISION FOR HIS CHILDREN.

Not only is sanctification the provision of God for His children, it is Christ's PRAYER for His spiritual brothers and sisters. *"These words spake Jesus, and lifted up his eyes to heaven, and said, Father . . . I have manifested Thy name unto the men which Thou gavest Me out of the world: Thine they were, and Thou gavest them Me; and they have kept Thy word . . . I pray for them . . . I pray not that Thou shouldest take them out of the world, but that Thou shouldest keep them from the evil. They are not of the world, even as I am not of the world. Sanctify them through Thy truth: Thy word is truth . . . Neither pray I for these alone, but for them also which shall believe on Me through their word"* (John 17:1a,6,9a,15-17,20).

How wonderfully this truth is brought out in the next personality found working on the **FOUNTAIN GATE**. *"Palal"* (Nehemiah 3:25) comes from a root word which can be translated two ways: "To judge," and "To pray, to intercede."

Many times when we think of judgment, we have the tendency to dwell on the negative, but the Bible teaches that God's Plan Of Redemption involves passing judgment in favor of His children, and Jesus is even now continuing to intercede in the Heavenly Sanctuary as our Great High Priest that this may be a reality.

Paul was so assured of the importance of prayer relative to sanctification that he left wise counsel for the church awaiting the Second Coming of Jesus. *"Abstain from all appearance of evil. And the very God of peace sanctify you wholly; and I pray God your whole spirit and soul and body be preserved blameless unto the coming of our Lord Jesus Christ"* (I Thessalonians 5:22,23).

Satan does not want us to do God's Will. Our enemy constantly seeks ways to lead us into trespasses. Because Jesus knows the tactics of the adversary, He encourages us to pray this type of prayer, as recorded in Matthew 6:9-13. *"After this manner therefore pray ye: Our Father Which art in heaven, Hallowed be Thy name. Thy kingdom come. Thy will be done in earth, as it is in heaven. Give us this day our daily bread. And forgive us our debts, as we forgive our debtors. And lead us not into temptation, but deliver us from evil: For Thine is the kingdom, and the power, and the glory, for ever. Amen."*

In so many ways, at so many places, during so many times, Satan works on our flesh so that we might slip and fall. Is it little wonder that Christ left this supplication for us to practice? *"Watch and pray, that ye enter not into temptation: the spirit indeed is willing, but the flesh is weak"* (Matthew 26:41).

The last personality who labored on the **FOUNTAIN GATE** should cause each of God's children to resound a hearty "PRAISE THE NAME OF THE LORD." His name was *"Pedaiah"* (Nehemiah 3:25), and his name means "God has ransomed, released, redeemed, rescued."

The entire Bible is a Statement of God's ability to redeem His creation, but in closing this study of the **FOUNTAIN GATE**, let us be reminded of one passage which sums up the Message and Mission of Jesus. It is found in Acts 26. Paul is delivering a defense before king Agrippa. After relating his early zeal to destroy the followers of Christ, lets pick up the story as Paul travels toward Damascus to persecute Christians, to destroy the followers of Christ: *"At midday, O king, I saw in the way a light from heaven, above the brightness of the sun, shining round about me and them which journeyed with me. And when we were all fallen to the earth, I heard a voice speaking unto me, and saying in the Hebrew tongue, Saul, Saul, why persecutest thou Me? it is hard for thee to kick against the pricks. And I said, Who art Thou, Lord? And He said, I am Jesus whom thou persecutest. But rise, and stand upon thy feet: for I have appeared unto thee for this purpose, to make thee a minister and a witness both of these things which thou hast seen, and of those things in the which I will appear unto thee; Delivering thee from the people, and from the Gentiles, unto whom now I send thee, To open their eyes, and to turn them from darkness to light, and from the power of Satan unto God, that they may receive forgiveness of sins, and inheritance among them which are sanctified by faith that is in Me"* (Acts 26:13-18).

Continually we can thank God for the **FOUNTAIN GATE**. It assures us that we can have our eyes opened. It assures us that we can be turned from darkness to light. It assures us that we can be turned from the power of Satan unto God. It assures us that we may receive forgiveness of sins. It assures us that we can receive an inheritance among them which are sanctified by faith. The **FOUNTAIN GATE** assures us that it is all "IN" Jesus!

No wonder the song writer thrilled to pen the words:

"Redeemed! And so happy in Jesus! No language my rapture can tell;
I know that the light of His presence, With me doth continually dwell.
Redeemed, Redeemed, Redeemed by the blood of the Lamb!
Redeemed, Redeemed, His child, and forever I am."

Chapter Seven

THE WATER GATE

*"Moveover the Nethinims dwelt in Ophel, unto the place over against the **water gate** toward the east, and the tower that lieth out. After them the Tekoites repaired another piece, over against the great tower that lieth out, even unto the wall of Ophel."*

(Nehemiah 3:26,27)

The **WATER GATE** Spiritually Signifies the **Baptism Of The Holy Spirit.** That the Holy Spirit Baptism is an important consideration in regard to God's Will for His children, is quite evident in the fact that the Holy Spirit is mentioned more than two hundred and sixty times in the New Testament.

Joel was inspired to liken the Holy Spirit Baptism unto water or liquid substance. *"And it shall come to pass afterward, that I* (God) *will pour out My spirit upon all flesh; and your sons and your daughters shall prophesy, your old men shall dream dreams, your young men shall see visions: And also upon the servants and upon the handmaids in those days will I pour out My spirit"* (Joel 2:28,29).

In the Scriptures, water was used for baptism. John the Baptist spoke on this issue as he preached a Message Of Hope to his generation: *"I indeed baptize you with water unto repentance"* (Matthew 3:11a).

And yet, in this very verse, is recorded John prophesying of another "Baptism" to be administered by Christ: *" . . . but He* (Messiah) *that cometh after me is mightier than I, Whose shoes I am not worthy to bear: He shall baptize you with the Holy Ghost, and with fire"* (Matthew 3:11b).

And so, it is very evident that this other "Baptism," is subsequent to repentance and the external sign of "water baptism" taking place to indicate that a New Birth has taken place, and so this other "Baptism" is not to be confused with or equated to "water baptism."

On the Day Of Pentecost, the words used to describe what transpired are unique to water or liquid substance, just as Joel and John prophesied. *"And suddenly there came a sound from heaven as of a rushing mighty wind, and it filled all the house where they were sitting . . . And they were all filled with the Holy Ghost, and began to speak with other tongues, as the Spirit gave them utterance"* (Acts 2:2,4).

Before going farther we need to be reminded that each **GATE** we are studying is directly linked to the preceding **GATES**, in Spiritual Context. The **GATES** are indeed **"GATEWAYS TO GLORY**." It is not by mistake that the **WATER GATE** follows the **FOUNTAIN GATE**. The process of "Sanctification" must have started in a person's life before that individual can be filled with God's Spirit because God's Spirit will not dwell in an unclean vessel. Paul was inspired to deal extensively with this principle in the following passages:

I Corinthians 3:16,17. *"Know ye not that ye are the temple of God, and that the Spirit of God dwelleth in you? If any man defile the temple of God, him shall God destroy; for the temple of God is holy, which temple ye are."*

I Corinthians 6:15-20. *"Know ye not that your bodies are the members of Christ? Shall I then take the members of Christ, and make them the members of an harlot? God forbid. What? Know ye not that he which is joined to an harlot is one body? For two, saith He, shall be one flesh. But he that is joined unto the Lord is one spirit. Flee fornication. Every sin that a man doeth is without the body; but he that committeth fornication sinneth against his own body. What? Know ye not that your body is the temple of the Holy Ghost which is in you, which ye have of God, and ye are not your own? For ye are bought with a price: therefore glorify God in your body, and in your spirit, which are God's."*

II Corinthians 6:16-7:1. *"And what agreement hath the temple of God with idols? For ye are the temple of the living God; as God hath said, I will dwell in them, and walk in them; and I will be their God, and they shall be My people. Wherefore come out from among them, and be ye separate, saith the Lord, and touch not the unclean thing; and I will receive you, And will be a Father unto you, and ye shall be My sons and daughters, saith the Lord Almighty. Having therefore these promises, dearly beloved, let us cleanse ourselves from all filthiness of the flesh and spirit, perfecting holiness in the fear of God."*

There are two groups of personalities mentioned relative to the **WATER GATE**: the *"Nethinims"* (Nehemiah 3:26); and the *"Tekoites"* (Nehemiah 3:27).

The Nethinims lived in Ophel, which was a mound or high piece of ground in Jerusalem. Nethinim means "one given."

To fully appreciate this fact, there are at least two aspects that must be explored and accepted.

First, God's Holy Spirit has been "given" as a witness to us. Second, God's Holy Spirit has been "given" to enable us to witness to others.

Let's notice the first aspect by looking at Hebrews 10:14-17. *"For by one offering He hath perfected for ever them that are sanctified. Whereof the Holy Ghost also is a witness to us: for after that He had said before, This is the covenant that I will make with them after those days, saith the Lord, I will put My laws into their hearts, and in their minds will I write them . . . And their sins and iniquities will I remember no more."*

That God has "given" His Holy Spirit affords assurance that God has accepted the sinless life, the atoning death, the liberating resurrection, and the interceding present ministry of His Son, Jesus Christ, to meet the requirements of justice and righteousness, so that we can, by faith, be forgiven of our sins.

There seems to be confusion with some concerning this point in conjunction with the Old Testament and New Testament. The confusion is cleared up when it is understood that in the Old Testament, God's Holy Spirit appeared to men, worked upon men, and empowered men, but did so **from without inward**. There was not the abiding in them as is the case in the New Testament. In the New Testament, the Holy Spirit works **from within outward**.

The "giving" was quite different in the Old Testament when compared to the New Testament. We might say that the Old Testament "giving" served as the PREPARATION, so as to pave the way for the POSSESSION which began to take place in the New Testament.

In the Old Testament the sins and iniquities of the people were forgiven as they observed the laws written upon stone and offered sacrifices. Now, the Holy Spirit puts God's laws into our hearts and minds, and we are assured of the efficacy of ONE OFFERING – the death of Jesus.

Aren't you glad for this witness?

Also, we need to understand, in conjunction with this, that The Holy Spirit Baptism is a GIFT. This Baptism cannot be earned, it cannot be bought, it cannot be received through physical blood lineage. The Holy Spirit Baptism is a GIFT. *"In the last day, that great day of the feast, Jesus stood and cried, saying, If any man thirst, let him come unto Me, and drink. He that believeth on Me, as the Scripture hath said, out of his belly shall flow rivers of living water. (But this spake He of the Spirit, which they that believe on Him should receive: for the Holy Ghost was not yet given; because that Jesus was not yet glorified)."* John 7:37-39.

Jesus later would pray for this future "giving" to take place. *"And I will pray the Father, and He shall give you another Comforter, that He may abide with you for ever; Even the Spirit of truth; Whom the world cannot receive, because it seeth Him not, neither knoweth Him: but ye know Him; for He dwelleth with you, and shall be in you"* (John 14:16,17).

On the Day Of Pentecost, the followers of Christ were filled with the Holy Spirit and some of the people asked in Acts 2:12, "*. . . What meaneth this?*" They did not have to wait long for the answer to their question – "*Peter, standing up with the eleven, lifted up his voice, and said unto them, Ye men of Judaea, and all ye that dwell at Jerusalem, be this known unto you, and hearken to my words . . . this is that which was spoken by the prophet Joel; And it shall come to pass in the last days, saith God, I will pour out of My Spirit upon all flesh: and your sons and your daughters shall prophesy, and your young men shall see visions, and your old men shall dream dreams: And on My servants and on My handmaidens I will pour out in those days of My Spirit; and they shall prophesy*" (Acts 2:14-18).

Peter and the other followers of Christ then shared God's Plan Of Salvation, that was even known by David: "*Men and brethren, let me freely speak unto you of the patriarch David, that he is both dead and buried, and his sepulchre is with us unto this day. Therefore being a prophet, and knowing that God had sworn with an oath to him, that of the fruit of his loins, according to the flesh, He would raise up Christ to sit on his throne; He seeing this before spake of the resurrection of Christ . . . This Jesus hath God raised up, whereof we all are witnesses. Therefore being by the right hand of God exalted, and having received of the Father the promise of the Holy Ghost, He hath shed forth this, which ye now see and hear . . . Therefore let all the house of Israel know assuredly, that God hath made that same Jesus, whom ye have crucified, both Lord and Christ*" (Acts 2:29-33,36).

How exciting it is to observe the response of the sincere in heart and mind to the message of the disciples. The response is recorded immediately in Acts 2:37-41. "*Now when they heard this, they were pricked in their heart, and said unto Peter and to the rest of the apostles, Men and brethren, what shall we do? Then Peter said unto them, Repent, and be baptized every one of you in the name of Jesus Christ for the remission of sins, and ye shall receive the gift of the Holy Ghost. For the promise is unto you, and to your children, and to all that are afar off, even as many as the Lord our God shall call.*

And with many other words did he testify and exhort, saying, Save yourselves from this untoward generation. Then they that gladly received his word were baptized: and the same day there were added unto them about three thousand souls."

Second, God has "given" His Holy Spirit so that we may be witnesses to others.

This is vividly seen in the other group which labored on the **WATER GATE**, the *"Tekoites."* Tekoites means "trumpets." It is also important that we see them in the context of the setting. Nehemiah 3:27, records, *"After them the Tekoites repaired another piece . . ."*

If you remember, the Tekoites were also involved in the construction of the **FISH GATE** (Nehemiah 3:5), which Spiritually Signifies, "Soulwinning" – sharing the Gospel of Jesus which is able to convert lost humanity.

When Jesus met with His followers after the Resurrection and gave them instruction to gather together in the Upper Room, He foretold that they would soon become dynamic witnesses of His Grace: *". . . ye shall receive power, after that the Holy Ghost is come upon you: and ye shall be witnesses unto Me both in Jerusalem, and in all Judaea, and in Samaria, and unto the uttermost part of the earth"* (Acts 1:8).

From the Upper Room emerged a mighty organism that pulsated with purpose – that being to boldly speak a Message Of Hope to a hopeless generation. In just a few years it was reported that the followers of Christ were indeed succeeding in the Power of God's Holy Spirit to accomplish His purpose for their being witnesses unto the uttermost part of the earth. It is recorded that they *". . . turned the world upside down . . . "* (Acts 17:6).

We have come a long way since those early days of the church, and many things have changed, but the desire of Jesus for us to be His witnesses has remained constant. In these last days, it is God's intention that we be empowered through the Baptism Of His Holy Spirit. When we as individuals and as the corporate body of Christ are filled with God's Holy Spirit, there will be at least two manifestations in relation to our being effective witnesses.

First, There Will Be A Revival Of Powerful, Persuasive, Public Preaching. *"But Peter, standing up with the eleven, lifted up his voice, and said unto them, Ye men of Judaea, and all ye that dwell at Jerusalem, be this known unto you, and hearken to my words . . . And with many other words did he testify and exhort, saying, Save yourselves from this untoward generation"* (Acts 2:14,40). Some are advocating that the day of public preaching is past, but the Bible does not support such a concept. I Corinthians 1:18,21, is still truth relevant for our generation, just as it was for that of Paul – *"For the preaching of the cross is to them that perish foolishness; but unto us which are saved it is the power of God . . . For after that in the wisdom of God the world by wisdom knew not God, it pleased God by the foolishness of preaching to save them that believe."*

Second, There Will Be A Revival Of House To House Witnessing. What happened in Acts 2:46,47, will happen in the closing hours of earth's history – *"And they, continuing daily with one accord in the temple, and breaking bread from house to house, did eat their meat with gladness and singleness of heart, Praising God, and having favour with all the people. And the Lord added to the church daily such as should be saved."*

Some within the church voice, with either word or action, that the work of witnessing is for the pastor or evangelist. But God has called every member of His church to share our faith with others.

Often the church is eager to support foreign missions and this is certainly important, but at the same time, there are mission fields, right next door, that need our attention. Oh, that we could grasp the concept of "ripple evangelism" – casting the Bread Of Life upon the sea of people where we are and allowing the ripple to spread it to the shores of distant hearts and minds. This is what Jesus had in mind when He told the disciples that their witnessing must first begin in Jerusalem, and spread eventually to the uttermost part of the earth.

The church needs and will be "given" a miracle touch from the Master, the empowering Baptism Of God's Holy Spirit, so that our vision may be anointed to have the same 20/20 clearness which characterized the early church. This 20/20 VISION is explained in Acts 20:20. The apostle testifies, *"And how I kept back nothing that was profitable unto you, but have shewed you, and have taught you* ***publicly****, and* ***from house to house****, Testifying both to the Jews, and also to the Greeks, repentance toward God, and faith toward our Lord Jesus Christ. And now, behold, I go bound in the spirit unto Jerusalem, not knowing the things that shall befall me there: Save that the Holy Ghost witnesseth in every city, saying that bonds and afflictions abide me. But none of these things move me, neither count I my life dear unto myself, so that I might finish my course with joy, and the ministry, which I have received of the Lord Jesus, to testify the gospel of the grace of God"* (Acts 20:20-24).

Chapter Eight

THE HORSE GATE

*"From above the **horse gate** repaired the priests, every one over against his house."*

(Nehemiah 3:28)

The Spiritual Significance of the **HORSE GATE**, is that of **service**. Throughout the Bible, the most striking feature in the references of the horse is the application to service and warlike purposes.

That the **HORSE GATE** follows the **WATER GATE** is of significant importance because it empowers one to be enabled to not only rightfully serve, but also to function *"as a good soldier of Jesus Christ"* (II Timothy 2:3). Far too often, attempts are made in one's own strength and power, but God repeatedly says to His children that our service journey is *"not by might, nor by power, but by My Spirit, saith the Lord of hosts"* (Zechariah 4:6).

This was the lesson Paul desired to convey to Timothy and to all others, because he had learned it well in his walk with Jesus. Back to II Timothy 2:3 – *"Thou therefore endure hardness, as a good soldier of Jesus Christ."* And almost as if in anticipation of Timothy asking how this could possibly be a reality, Paul has already diffused anticipation in chapter 1:8. *"Be not thou therefore ashamed of the testimony of our Lord, nor of me His prisoner: but be thou partaker of the afflictions of the gospel according to the power of God."* Paul then proceeded to talk about being able to overcome in the strength of *"the Holy Ghost Which dwelleth in us"* (II Timothy 1:14).

It is very interesting that the group which repaired the **HORSE GATE** was that of *"the priests."* To better understand the Spiritual Significance of the **HORSE GATE**, we need to take a brief look at the priesthood as depicted in the Scriptures and how it related to service and spiritual warfare.

After Israel left the land of Egypt and began the journey toward the Promised Land of Canaan, God gave instruction for the construction of the Tabernacle, which was to be a most vital part of their success – both spiritually and physically. As part of the ongoing function, a priesthood was established so that it might perform certain responsibilities and privileges to insure communion between the people and their God.

The priesthood, according to Exodus 28, consisted of Aaron (the brother of Moses) and his sons. Their role was explicitly outlined. God said they were to *"minister unto Me in the priest's office"* (Exodus 28:3).

As part of the ceremony *"to hallow them"* (Exodus 29:1), or to consecrate them, God gave this commandment: *"Then shalt thou take the anointing oil, and pour it upon his head, and anoint him."* In the Scriptures, oil symbolizes the Spirit of God. And so, we see from the establishing of the priesthood how important it is to be empowered with God's Spirit in order to be an efficient, effective servant. By the way (and this is very crucial), in translating the word "minister," one should understand that it definitely is interchangeable with our word "servant." In other words, we can say that the priests were empowered or equipped by God's Spirit to function as servants of the people in their service of God.

In Numbers 3, we discover that the priesthood was expanded. Two of the sons of Aaron violated their position and *"offered strange fire before the Lord"* (verse 3). As a result, they died. Without spending too much time on this point, it is very interesting that in Acts 2, fire was a part of the Spiritual Baptism which took place on the Day of Pentecost. Without question, it is dangerous to attempt to substitute our efforts (strange fire) for the empowerment (true fire) of God's Spirit. Again, it must be emphasized that the **WATER GATE** empowers one to rightly serve.

Aware that the task of a Tabernacle-related ministry was too great for just Aaron and his two remaining sons, God gave permission for the priesthood to be expanded. *"And the Lord spake unto Moses, saying, Bring the tribe of Levi near, and present them before Aaron the priest, that they may minister unto him. And they shall keep his charge, and the charge of the whole congregation before the tabernacle of the congregation, to do the service of the tabernacle. And they shall keep all the instruments of the tabernacle of the congregation, and the charge of the children of Israel, to do the service of the tabernacle. And thou shalt give the Levites unto Aaron and to his sons: they are wholly given unto him out of the children of Israel"* (Numbers 3:5-9).

The tribe of Levi was incorporated into the priesthood. They were to: 1. Minister unto God; 2. Minister unto Aaron; 3. Do the service of the Tabernacle. Numbers 8:11, explains how their ministry – their priesthood was intended by God to convey a message to the people of Israel. They were called and commissioned so *"that they may execute the service of the Lord."*

In the New Testament, the priesthood was again expanded. John afforded the insight that because Christ *"loved us, and washed us from our sins in His own blood"* (Revelation 1:5), He has *"made us kings and priests unto God and His Father; to Him be glory and dominion for ever and ever"* (Revelation 1:6).

Every believer in Jesus Christ is now incorporated into the priesthood. This is sometimes referred to as the Priesthood Of The Believer. This concept was not unique to John; it was understood by the early New Testament Church in general. Peter referred to believers in Christ, even though we may be *"newborn babes"* (I Peter 2:2), as *"a holy priesthood"* (I Peter 2:5) – a *"royal priesthood"* (I Peter 2:9).

The fact that this incorporation of the believer into the priesthood of God is His will now for us is clearly shared in Revelation 5:9,10, where it is stated that Christ, the Lamb, " . . . *was slain, and hast redeemed us to God by* (His) *blood out of every kindred, and tongue, and people, and nation; And hast made us unto our God kings and priests: and we shall reign on the earth."*

And why have we been called and commissioned as priests? So that we may effectively *"execute the service of the Lord"* (Numbers 8:11).

The **HORSE GATE** life of SERVICE is the Grand Privilege of each Christian. To be sure it is our obligation, but we also must practice it as our privilege. Jesus spoke words that establish this principle in Luke 17.

In verses 7 and 8, He cast light on the servant-master relationship – the servant is to serve the master. *"But which of you, having a servant plowing or feeding cattle, will say unto him by and by, when he is come from the field, Go and sit down to meat? And will not rather say unto him, Make ready wherewith I may sup, and gird thyself, and serve me, till I have eaten and drunken; and afterward thou shalt ear and drink?"*

Jesus then asked the question of the disciples and then gave His own response: *"Doth he* (the master) *thank that servant because he did the things that were commanded him? I trow* (think) *not"* (verse 9).

Before the disciples could raise objections or ask why, Christ continued: *"So likewise ye,* (inferring them to be servants) *when ye shall have done all those things which are commanded you, say, We are unprofitable servants . . ."* (Verse 10a). Literally, what He is saying is that they should consider themselves deserving of no special commendation.

Some seem confused on this matter as they give the impression or even state with actions and words that they want others, and even God, to constantly pat them on the head so all can see they are special and say "thank you." However, the opposite should be our attitude – we should be thanking God. Why? Because when everything is said and done, *"we are unprofitable servants"* – we are worthy only through faith in and commitment to the Master.

To adopt this kind of philosophy and practice will enable us to rejoice in, rather than resist against, the following words of Jesus: *"say . . .* ***we have done that which was our duty to do."***

The Christian who has walked through the previous **GATES** and accepted THEIR CONTENT will indeed recognize **service** as Our Grand Privilege – it is that which is our duty to do. Paul practiced this and encouraged others to allow it to be their lifestyle as well. He talked of it being our *"reasonable service"* (Romans 12:1). In writing to Timothy he used himself as an example of encouragement: *"And I thank Christ Jesus our Lord, Who hath enabled me, for that he counted me faithful, putting me into the ministry . . . This charge I commit unto thee, son Timothy . . . that thou . . . mightest war a good warfare"* (I Timothy 1:12,18).

Paul was enabled or empowered because of the **WATER GATE** to serve (**HORSE GATE**) and he desired that Timothy – that you and I – also adopt the Grand Privilege Of Service. We are in a war just as was he and Timothy, just as has been every soldier of Christ and the way we come through victorious is to be like Jesus, Who *"made Himself of no reputation, and took upon Him the form of a servant . . . "* (Philippians 2:7).

Perhaps our study on the **HORSE GATE** can be summed up in this admonition: *"Servants, be obedient to them that are your masters according to the flesh, with fear and trembling, in singleness of your heart, as unto Christ; Not with eye-service, as men-pleasers; but as the servants of Christ, doing the will of God from the heart; With good will doing service as to the Lord, and not to men: Knowing that whatsoever good thin any man doeth, the same shall he receive of the Lord, whether he be bond or free . . . be strong in the Lord, and in the power of His might. Put on the whole armour of God, that ye may be able to stand against the wiles of the devil. For we wrestle not against flesh and blood, but against principalities, against powers, against rules of the darkness of this world, against spiritual wickedness in high places. Wherefore take unto you the whole armour of God, that ye may be able to withstand in the evil day, and having done all, to stand"* (Ephesians 6:5-8; 10-13).

I repeat: God has called and commissioned each of His children to be a priest. Why? So that we may effectively *"execute the service of the Lord"* (Numbers 8:11).

Chapter Nine

THE EAST GATE

"After them repaired Zadok the son of Immer over against his house. After him repaired also Shemaiah the son of Shechaniah, the keeper of the ***east gate.****"*
(Nehemiah 3:29)

The **EAST GATE** Spiritually Signifies the **hope of the blessed Second Coming of our Lord and Saviour Jesus Christ.** It is interesting to note how often **"east"** is linked in the Scriptures with the Second Coming.

Matthew 24:27. *"For as the lightening cometh out of the east, and shineth even unto the west; so shall also the coming of the Son of man be."*

Acts 1:11. After His Resurrection, Jesus ascended from the Mount of Olives, which was a ridge east of Jerusalem. Two heavenly messengers said to the disciples who witnessed His ascension: *"Ye men of Galilee, why stand ye gazing up into Heaven? This same Jesus, which is taken up from you into Heaven, shall so come in like manner as ye have seen Him go into Heaven."*

Zechariah 14:4. At the Battle of Armageddon, which is connected with Christ's Second Coming, *"His feet shall stand in that day upon the Mount of Olives, which is before Jerusalem on the east . . . "*

There were two personalities who were involved in the construction of the **EAST GATE**: *"Zadok"* and *"Shemaiah."*

Zadok means "righteous." Shemaiah comes from a root word which means "to hear with attention, to hear with obedience, to hear with the attitude of coming together."

Both of those meanings are very important in the Second Coming, because God is calling for a righteous people to meet His Son – God is calling us to hear what Jesus would say to us with attention and obedience so as to come together in one mind and one accord in order that we will be ready to meet Him with clean hands and a pure heart.

Ever since His death, resurrection and ascension, the followers of Christ have talked about and looked forward to the coming of Jesus. We are living in a very technological age which is allowing us to make rapid changes in so many areas.

A question each person must ask is: when we consider the changes in which we are involved, is it still important for Christians to look with expectation for the Second Coming of Jesus? Or have we out grown that theology? Is it still important to look for One Who will give us "The New Age?" Is there a need in our technological age for a fresh, and renewed call to be made concerning the nearness of end-time Bible Prophecy to be fulfilled? Is there a need for us to proclaim with lip and life that God will indeed send His Son to receive in glorious fashion those who have passed the test of life?

I John 3:1 – *"Behold, what manner of love the Father hath bestowed upon us, that we should be called the sons of God: therefore the world knoweth us not, because it knew Him not."* The world has become too well acquainted with us. The world has determined, by and large, what strings can be pulled to get our attention. God said that because we are His children, the world should not know us because it knew Him not.

John was inspired to continue in verse 2: *"Beloved, now are we the sons of God, and it doth not yet appear what we shall be: but we know that, when He shall appear, we shall be like Him . . . "* Does this mean that when Jesus returns we will all of a sudden be changed and be like Him then, or does it mean that if we are not like Jesus before He returns, we will not know Jesus when He returns?

How do we see Jesus? Are we looking for Jesus in the sweet-by-and-by, or are we looking for Jesus today? What kind of philosophy do we have about Him? Do we see Jesus as He was and as He is?

Notice what happens when a person has a proper perspective of Jesus and His Coming: *"And every man that hath this hope in him purifieth himself, even as He is pure"* (verse 3). What hope is this speaking of? The appearing or Second Coming of Jesus. And when we have this HOPE IN Jesus, it places us in a position that Jesus can do something for us – so, in a sense, we have a role to play in the amount of purification we experience. It is by surrendering to His Lordship – It is by surrendering to His Righteousness – It is by surrendering in obedience to His Word – It is by surrendering to His summons to come together in His grace. The Second Coming is indeed a part of our Purifying Hope.

TWO QUESTIONS Need To Be Asked And Addressed:

First Question: Why has Jesus not returned?

This is a question I have asked others and has been asked of me. Can it be – can it really be that Christ is waiting with longing desire for the manifestation of Himself in His church? I John 3:1-3, and many other passages teach that when the character of Christ is reproduced in His people, then He will return to claim them as His own. *"Behold, what manner of love the Father hath bestowed upon us, that we should be called the sons of God: therefore the world knoweth us not, because it knew Him not. Beloved, now are we the sons of God, and it doth not yet appear what we shall be: but we know that, when He shall appear, we shall be like Him; for we shall see Him as He is. And every man that hath this hope in Him purifieth himself, even as He is pure."* Can it be – can it really be that if we longed for Jesus to return as much as Jesus longs to return for us that we would soon be with Him in Heaven?

Revelation 3:14-17, gives us emphatic insight into this area of concern. Jesus is addressing, through John the local church of Laodicea, which represented the last church age which would live just prior to His Second Coming. This is what He says: *"And unto the angel of the church of the Laodiceans write; These things saith the*

Amen, the faithful and true witness, the beginning of the creation of God; I know thy works, that thou are neither cold nor hot: I would thou wert cold or hot. So then because thou are lukewarm, and neither cold nor hot, I will spue thee out of My mouth. Because thou sayest, I am rich, and increased with goods, and have need of nothing; and knowest not that thou art wretched, and miserable, and poor, and blind, and naked: I counsel thee to buy of Me gold tried in the fire, that thou mayest be rich; and white raiment, that thou mayest be clothed, and that the shame of thy nakedness do not appear; and anoint thine eyes with eye-salve, that thou mayest see. As many as I love, I rebuke and chasten: be zealous therefore, and repent. Behold, I stand at the door, and knock: if any man hear My voice, and open the door, I will come in to him, and will sup with him, and he with Me. To him that overcometh will I grant to sit with Me in My throne, even as I also overcame, and am set down with My Father in His throne. He that hath an ear, let him hear what the Spirit saith unto the churches."

Jesus has not returned, He testifies (as the *"True Witness"*), because there is prevailing in our church age the philosophy, mentality, and practice of Laodicea. Remember the two personalities who labored on the **EAST GATE**? Zadok ("righteous"), and Shemaiah ("to hear with obedience"). It is impossible to read the message of Jesus for Laodicea (our church age, if you will) and not sense His urgent plea that we experience change relative to "righteous" and exercise "obedience through hearing" what He says to us through His Spirit.

Two characteristics of Laodicea are spelled out in these verses which are preventing Jesus from returning:

1. A Synthesizing Of Ideas (*"I know thy works, that thou art neither cold nor hot: I would thou wert cold or hot"* – verse 15). Jesus termed this synthesizing of ideas, *"lukewarmness."* Probably a word we would better understand in our modern vernacular would be that of COMPROMISE. We as a church have moved, to a great degree, into an era of compromise. There was a time in the history of the church when things were black or white relative to principle and

conviction. There was a time when things were either sin or not sin. But we have moved into an era when there is lacking of a forceful voice which talks about sin – there is a breakdown in a forceful call for righteousness. And we need to notice that this kind of call does not have to be mean and vengeful. The call for a revival can and must be made in love (*"As many as I love, I rebuke and chasten: be zealous therefore, and repent"* – verse 19).

It seems as though most everything has been thrown into the caldron and has emerged as grey. We do what is right in our own eyes. Jesus has not changed – we are the ones who have changed relative to our perception and practice. There is a great need for men, women, and youth who will resound with lips and radiate with life: *"as for me and my house, we will serve God"* (Joshua 24:15).

The desire of Christ is for us to be on either one side of the fence or the other. He has no desire or respect for our attempts to "FENCE-STRADDLE." He desires for us to take a stand – either for Him or against Him. The person who stands for nothing lives in a state of compromise – is lukewarm – is neither hot nor cold – will fall for anything and in the end will lose everything.

2. A Prevailing Spirit And Attitude Of Self-Exaltation (verse 17). Jesus testified that the prevailing concept of self was and would be: *"I am rich, and increased with goods, and have need of nothing."* Probably a word we would better understand in our modern vernacular would be that of "humanism."

It is sad how there seems to be a growing promotion of personality within the church – looking for exaltation, either consciously or unconsciously. The Bible says that we should take heed when we think we stand lest we fall (I Corinthians 10:12). When we begin to focus on ourselves and take our eyes away from Jesus, we stand in jeopardy of a tremendous disappointment and fall.

The trap of Satan has not changed. He is full aware of our weakness and his past experience of victories with the human family gives him confidence that it is a trap capable of ensnaring again and again and again. How sad that too many (and just one is too many, because God so loved that He sent Jesus that all – whosoever will might not perish) do not understand the destruction which awaits.

This is why the **GATEWAYS TO GLORY** are so important. They serve as an ongoing reminder that Jesus came the First Time in order to save us from the Power and Penalty of sin; and He is going to return the Second time in order to save us from the Presence of sin.

Second Question: What will bring Jesus back?

REPENTANCE. Nothing else. We must come to the place where we not only recognize, but also are willing to confess that we have sinned and come short of God's Will for our lives and living through our compromising of principle and our exaltation of self. What will bring Jesus back? Crying out in repentant remorse: "Forgive me God for the sinfulness of my way."

Of the seven churches mention in Revelation 2 and 3, only two of them escaped a rebuke from Jesus – five came under condemnation. It is imperative that we notice and absorb the message Jesus gave each of the five churches who were in trouble. The message was the same to each:

Revelation 2:5	Repent
Revelation 2:16	Repent
Revelation 2:21,22	Repent
Revelation 3:3	Repent
Revelation 3:19	Repent

What will bring Jesus back? A Revival Of **REPENTANCE**.

In Mark 13, Jesus spoke to His generation and it was preserved for ours in order that we might also learn this much needed lesson. *"But of that day and that hour knoweth no man* (referring to His Second Coming)*, no not the angels which are in heaven, neither the Son, but the Father. Take heed, watch and pray, for ye know not when the time is. For the Son of man is as a man taking a far journey, who left his house, and gave authority to his servants, and to every man his work,* *and commanded the porter to watch. Watch ye therefore: for ye know not when the Master of the house cometh, at even, or at midnight, or at the cockcrowing, or in the morning: Lest coming suddenly He find you sleeping. And what I say unto you I say unto all, Watch"* (verses 32-37).

Why did Jesus admonish that we should take heed, watch and pray? Very simple answer: There Is A Purifying Essence Involved In Believing And Proclaiming The SECOND COMING Of Jesus Christ.

We need a revival of teaching and living the "DISTURBING DOCTRINE OF THE SECOND COMING OF JESUS." Why do I make the statement that the Second Coming of Jesus is a "Disturbing Doctrine?" Simply, because when we begin to live in anticipation of The Second Coming Of Jesus, we will see a transformation take place in our lives and in the lives of others – and this transformation will make Satan so angry that he will pull out all stops and the Great Controversy between good and evil will come to an abrupt end.

Once and for all, we need to settle in our minds and hearts the question of what type of church will welcome Jesus as King of kings and Lord of lords when He returns. Once and for all we need to settle the question of what type of church will be transplanted to God's Heaven when Christ returns the Second Time.

For what kind of church is Jesus Returning? Ephesians 5:25-27. *"Husbands, love your wives, even as Christ also loved the church, and gave Himself for it; That He might sanctify and cleanse it with the washing of water by the word, That He might present it to Himself a glorious church, not having spot, or wrinkle, or any such thing; but that it should be holy and without blemish."*

For what kind of church is Jesus Returning? II Peter 3:10-14. *"But the day of the Lord will come as a thief in the night; in the which the heavens shall pass away with a great noise, and the elements shall melt with fervent heat, the earth also and the works that are therein shall be burned up. Seeing then that all these things shall be dissolved, what manner of persons ought ye to be in all hold conversation and godliness, Looking for and hasting unto the* *coming of the day of God, wherein the heavens being on fire shall be dissolved, and the elements shall melt with fervent heat? Nevertheless we, according to His promise, look for new heavens and a new earth, wherein dwelleth righteousness. Wherefore, beloved, seeing that ye look for such things, be diligent that ye may be found of Him in peace, without spot, and blameless."*

For what kind of church is Jesus Returning? Titus 2:11-14. *"For the grace of God that bringeth salvation hath appeared to all men, teaching us that, denying ungodliness and worldly lusts, we should live soberly, righteously, and godly, in this present world; Looking for that blessed hope, and the glorious appearing of the great God and our Saviour Jesus Christ; Who gave Himself for us, that he might redeem us from all iniquity, and purify unto Himself a peculiar people, zealous of good works."*

If we want to be like Jesus in the world to come, we must be like Jesus in this *"present world"* – living *"righteously"* by faith as we are *"looking for that Blessed Hope"* – The Second Coming.

The **EAST GATE** is a reality. Jesus is Coming Again. The question is: Will we be ready to meet Him, to welcome Him and to crown Him with clean hands and pure hearts? It pains me to think that I could actually be part of the cause for the delay of Christ's Return. My prayer, and I hope you will join me in it is: Jesus, please forgive me and give me Your Spirit so that I may be victorious over sin and sinning for Your Name's Sake.

Chapter Ten

THE MIPHKAD GATE

"After him repaired Hananiah the son of Shelemiah, and Hanun the sixth son of Zalaph, another piece. After him repaired Meshullam the son of Berechiah over against his chamber. After him repaired Malchiah the goldsmith's son unto the place of the Nethinims, and of the merchants, over against the ***gate Miphkad****, and to the going up of the corner."*
(Nehemiah 3:30,31)

Spiritually speaking, the **GATE MIPHKAD**, signifies the **judgment which is related to the Second Coming of Jesus.**

"Miphkad" means: "A review appointment for judgment. An appointment or assignment concerning a designated spot, specifically, a census or appointed place."

One of the great, comforting truths that gives hope to every Christian is the knowledge that our Saviour, Jesus Christ, will also be involved in the judgment. To be sure, judgment is a serious consideration, but we can be assured that it will be passed in accord with both the mercy and justice of God. The judgment is not to be feared. It is to be viewed as part of Christ's plan for His Father's children.

To aid in appreciating the liberating quality of judgment, there are three questions we can explore. But before exploring these three questions, let's be reminded of the meaning of the four personalities who labored on the **MIPHKAD GATE**. We have seen these names before in others who labored on previous gates.

"Hananiah" means "whom God favors."
"Hanun" means "whom God pities."
"Meshullam" means "a friend."
"Malchiah" means "Jehovah is King."

As we look at the Spiritual Significance of the **MIPHKAD GATE**, the meaning of these names will take on much importance and perhaps give us a portrait of judgment which has, by and large, been missed by many of the Christian Church.

QUESTION ONE: Was Judgment A Part Of The Old Testament Day Of Atonement?

Under the sacrificial system of the Old Testament, when a person committed a sin, he took an offering to the priest, and after it was slain the priest symbolically transferred the sin inside the Sanctuary. Daily, blood was shed for the remission of sins, and the transgressions accumulated, as it was, inside the Sanctuary.

It is not difficult then, to see how the confessed sins which were transferred inside the Sanctuary could cause it to become defiled. But, God also included in the Old Testament Plan Of Redemption a remedy for ridding the Sanctuary of this condition. The remedy is outlined in Leviticus 16, and involved several elements. It is referred to as the Day Of Atonement, and took place once a year.

Before turning to that passage, let's notice briefly Hebrews 9:7, because it informs of the Day Of Atonement being related to ministry within the *"most holy place."*

"But into the second went the high priest alone once every year, not without blood, which he offered for himself, and for the errors of the people."

Now, to Leviticus 16. To the Israelite, the Day Of Atonement involved at least three areas:

(1) The Blotting Out Of Confessed Sins.

After the high priest had washed himself and put on the holy garments, he killed the bullock of sin offering, which was for himself, and sprinkled its blood upon the mercy seat (within the *"most holy place"*) with his finger seven times. He then killed a goat of sin offering, which was for the people, and followed the same procedure.

In so doing, the high priest was admitting that the law of God (which was in the ark of the covenant beneath the mercy seat) had been violated. The people and he had come seeking pardon for breaking God's commandments, and the blood was the agency for securing that pardon. As the blood was applied to the Sanctuary furnishings, the smoke from the censer filled with incense would cover the mercy seat and fill the Sanctuary with its sweet fragrance.

After the glory of God filled the Sanctuary, indicating the Lord's acceptance of the offering, the high priest came to the door and called for a second goat to be brought to him. Upon the head of this goat he laid his hands and confessed *"over him all the iniquities of the children of Israel, and all their transgressions in all their sins, putting them upon the head of the goat, and shall send him away by the hand of a fit man into the wilderness: And the goat shall bear upon him all their iniquities unto a land not inhabited: and he shall let go the goat in the wilderness"* (verses 20-22).

When the service was completed, the high priest came out of the Tabernacle and the people knew their record was clean. Their sins had been blotted out and placed, as it was, upon the "scapegoat." They were no longer held accountable. Look at verse 30 – *"For on that day shall the priest make an atonement for you, to cleanse you, that ye may be clean from all your sins before the Lord."*

So it is clear that the daily sacrifices were important, but the dailies were incomplete without the yearly Day Of Atonement application of the sacrificial blood to the accounts of the people.

(2) The Cleansing Of The Sanctuary.

Because the sins of the people had defiled the sanctuary during the year, it was necessary not only for the people to be cleansed, but also for the Sanctuary to be cleansed. This was to be accomplished with the shedding of blood. Let's read several verses to get this picture clearly imprinted in our minds and hearts. *"Then shall he kill the goat of the sin offering, that is for the people, and bring his blood within the veil, and do with that blood as he did with the blood of the bullock, and sprinkle it upon the mercy seat, and before the mercy seat: And he shall make an atonement for the holy place, because of the uncleanness of the children of Israel, and because of their transgressions in all their sins: and so shall he do for the tabernacle of the congregation, that remaineth among them in the midst of their uncleanness . . . And he shall go out unto the altar that is before the Lord, and make an atonement for it; and shall take of the blood of the bullock, and of the blood of the goat, and put it upon the horns of the altar round about. And he shall sprinkle of the blood upon it with his finger seven times, and cleanse it, and hallow it from the uncleanness of the children of Israel . . . And he shall make an atonement for the holy sanctuary, and he shall make an atonement for the tabernacle of the congregation, and for the altar, and he shall make an atonement for the priests, and for all the people of the congregation"* (Verses 15,16,18,19,33).

Thus, it is clear that on the Day Of Atonement, when the sins of the people were blotted out, the Sanctuary and altar were, at the same time, cleansed from the year's defilement.

(3) A Time Of Judgment **For** The People.

This was a most solemn day for Israel and was to be spent in self-examination as the people fasted and prayed. Verses 29-31, teach that the actions on the Day Of Atonement were of life and death consequences. In view of such gravity the people were instructed that they should *"afflict"* their souls. *"And this shall be a statute for ever unto you: that in the seventh month, on the tenth day of the month, ye shall afflict your souls, and do no work at all, whether it be one of your own country, or a stranger that sojourneth among you: For on that day shall the priest make an atonement for you, to cleanse you, that ye may be clean from all your sins before the Lord. It shall be a sabbath of rest unto you, and ye shall afflict your souls, by a statute for ever."*

To gain a more complete portrait of what this means, we need to notice Leviticus 23:26-32. *"And the Lord spake unto Moses, saying, Also on the tenth day of this seventh month there shall be a day of atonement: it shall be an holy convocation unto you; and ye shall afflict your souls, and offer an offering made by fire unto the Lord. And ye shall do no work in that same day: for it is a day of atonement, to make an atonement for you before the Lord your God. For whatsoever soul it be that shall not be afflicted in that same day, he shall be cut off from among his people. And whatsoever soul it be that doeth any work in that same day, the same soul will I destroy from among his people. Ye shall do no manner of work: it shall be a statute for ever throughout your generations in all your dwellings. It shall be unto you a sabbath of rest, and ye shall afflict your souls: in the ninth day of the month at even, from even unto even, shall ye celebrate your sabbath."*

We might say then, that the Day Of Atonement was a TIME OF JUDGMENT to prove who really believed in the Lord enough to obey His every command. Anyone who did not pass the test was to be *"cut off from among his people,"* and stood in jeopardy of being destroyed.

On the surface, such a time might seem to be austere or harsh, but all one has to do to see a positive side is to catch a glimpse of the glory involved. God's concern for His people – a people He favored (*"Hananiah"*) – a people He pitied (*"Hanun"*) – a people He desired to be His friend (*"Meshullam"*) – a people who needed to acknowledge Him as their King (*"Malchiah"*) – is vividly seen in verse 32. God wanted them to enter that day with joy and confidence of reward. *"It shall be unto you a sabbath of rest, and ye shall afflict your souls: in the ninth day of the month at even, from even unto even, shall ye celebrate your sabbath."*

QUESTION TWO: Is Judgment A Part Of The Present Atoning Ministry Of Christ?

By now, you may be wondering: What does all this have to do with Christ being involved in our judgment, and that the judgment is not to be feared, but is to be viewed as part of Christ's Plan for His Father's children?

Nehemiah three, informs us that the **GATE MIPHKAD** not only is related to the **EAST GATE** (which we discovered Spiritually Signifies the Second Coming of Jesus), but it is also related to the **SHEEP GATE** (verse 32). As you remember, our study began with this **GATE**, which Spiritually Signifies THE ATONEMENT, THE NEW BIRTH, BEING FORGIVEN OF SINS. We are making a full circle.

Our study has focused on **"THE GATEWAYS TO GOD'S GLORY,"** and the central ingredient is the desire of God to save *"whosoever will"* from the power of sin, the penalty of sin, and the presence of sin. You see, the judgment cannot be studied apart from the Atonement, because the Atonement (**THE SHEEP GATE**) gives us assurance that we are people *"whom God favors"* ("Hananiah"); people *"whom God pities"* ("Hanun"); people with whom God desires to be *"a friend"* ("Meshullam"); people who need to recognize *"Jehovah as King"* ("Malchiah").

Today, we are living in the autumn of time, and Revelation 14, gives us a glimpse of what will happen just before Jesus returns for. His people. There are three messages which are to be delivered in the last days.

Notice the first message found in Revelation 14:6,7. *"And I saw another angel fly in the midst of heaven, having the everlasting gospel to preach unto them that dwell on the earth, and to every nation, and kindred, and tongue, and people, Saying with a loud voice, Fear God, and give glory to Him; for* ***the hour of His judgment is come****: and worship Him that made heaven, and earth, and the sea, and the fountains of waters."*

As we read this chapter, it must be noted that the judgment hour is to come **BEFORE** the Second Coming of Christ. Verse 6, says *"the hour of His judgment is come,"* and the Second Coming is not mentioned until verse 14. *"And I looked, and behold a white cloud, and upon the cloud one sat like unto the Son of man, having on His head a golden crown, and in His hand a sharp sickle. And another angel came out of the temple, crying with a loud voice to Him that sat* *on the cloud, Thrust in Thy sickle, and reap: for the time is come for Thee to reap; for the harvest of the earth is ripe."*

We might say that it is to be a **pre-advent judgment**, and this judgment, according to Peter *"must begin at the house of God"* (I Peter 4:17).

Daniel, as did John, also gained insight in the relationship of Jesus to a **pre-advent judgment**. Daniel 7:9,10. *"I beheld till the thrones were cast down, and the Ancient of days did sit, whose garment was white as snow, and the hair of His head like the pure wool: His throne was like the fiery flame, and His wheels as burning fire. A fiery stream issued and came forth from before Him: thousand thousands ministered unto Him, and ten thousand times ten thousand stood before Him: the judgment was set, and the books were opened."*

As we read this chapter, it must again be noted that the judgment hour is to come **BEFORE** the Second Coming of Christ. Verse 10 says, *"the judgment was set and the books were opened,"* and the Second Coming is not mentioned until verses 13 and 14. *"I saw in the night visions, and, behold one like the Son of man came with the clouds of heaven, and came to the Ancient of days, and they brought Him near before Him. And there was given Him dominion, and glory, and a kingdom, that all people, nations, and languages, should serve Him: His dominion is an everlasting dominion, which shall not pass away, and His kingdom that which shall not be destroyed."*

If you will do a study on the Second Coming of Jesus, you will discover that the language of John and Daniel in using the picture of Him Returning ***with clouds*** is a theme woven throughout the Bible. Revelation 1:7; Acts 1:9-11; I Thessalonians 4:15-18; Matthew 24:29-31; Matthew 26:64; Mark 13:24-27; Mark 14:62.

Indeed, the Bible teaches that Jesus will be involved in a Ministry Of Judgment, and that this will indeed be a **pre-advent judgment**. To some, this concept causes some concern, because a very popular teaching about the judgment is that it will take place AFTER the Second Coming Of Jesus.

However, to rightfully understand the **MIPHKAD GATE**, a **"Pre-Advent Judgment"** gives the Christian and to the faithful angels a great assurance that there is no contradiction in the Bible as to the possibility of God making mistakes relative to rewards. Remember how we closed the study on the **EASE GATE**? We did so by viewing how our WORKS will be involved in our worthiness and readiness to welcome the Returning Christ.

Titus 2:11-14. *"For the grace of God that bringeth salvation hath appeared to all men, teaching us that, denying ungodliness and worldly lusts, we should live soberly, righteously, and godly, in this present world; Looking for that blessed hope, and the glorious appearing of the great God and our Saviour Jesus Christ; Who gave Himself for us, that he might redeem us from all iniquity, and purify unto Himself a peculiar people, zealous of good works."*

In Revelation 22:12, Jesus said to John and says to us: *"And behold, I come quickly; and My reward is with Me, to give every man according as his work shall be."*

I well remember struggling with the whole concept of a **"pre-advent judgment"** a number of years ago and the study I am sharing with you has given me great peace. You see, I came to understand that there has to be a STANDARD by which each of us will either be accepted or rejected – the STANDARD has to be the same for one and all. Also, I came to understand that in order to insure that neither angels nor the inheritors of Heaven never have any questions as to the worthiness of any individual being there, God will answer the questions before they can ever be asked. Thus – **PRE-ADVENT JUDGMENT**.

The case of every person will be reviewed and settled before Jesus returns and this is why He could say to John then, and reiterates to us today, ***"I come quickly; and My reward is with me**, to give every man according as his work shall be."* The very fact that we will receive a *"reward"* WHEN Jesus Returns, not only suggests, but PROVES that we will have **passed the test**. What test? The test of **PRE-ADVENT JUDGMENT**.

Paul understood this when he stated: *"For there is no respect of persons with God"* (Romans 2:11). The STANDARD is the same for all, and all will be judged on the basis of response (works) to the STANDARD. Let's continue listening: *"But we are sure that the judgment of God is according to truth . . . the revelation of the righteous judgment of God; Who will render to every man according to his deeds . . . "* (Romans 2:2-11). He then later gives enlightenment on this entire issue my stating that there will be a *"day when God shall judge the secrets of men by Jesus Christ according to* (the) *gospel"* (Romans 2:16).

QUESTION THREE: How Should We React To The Judgment?

Do you realize what all this means for you and me? Jesus is soon to return! When Jesus ascended after His resurrection He was seated at the side of His Father and assumed His High Priestly ministry of intercession in the Sanctuary of Heaven. Through the centuries the Plan Of Atonement has been shared by His followers through the anointing of His Holy Spirit, and multitudes have confessed their sins and asked for forgiveness. While it has not been necessary for Jesus to be re-crucified for each individual, His blood has been applied, the name of the repentant one written in a special book, and we are living in the fulfillment of a glorious time for the Christian.

Our High Priest is ministering in favor of those whose names have been written in the Book Of Life and live in obedience to the light they have received.

Soon Jesus is going to come out of the Heavenly Sanctuary and when He does, Revelation 22:10, 11, will become a reality, because the Day Of Atonement will have ended. *"...the time is at hand. He that is unjust, let him be unjust still: and he which is filthy, let him be filthy still: and he that is righteous, let him be righteous still: and he that is holy, let him be holy still."*

When the Day Of Atonement ends, the sins which have been forgiven through faith in the precious blood of the Lamb will all be placed on the shoulders of the old goat, Satan himself, and he will be bound a thousand years to think of the tragedy he has brought upon mankind.

JUDGMENT WILL HAVE BEEN PASSED IN FAVOR OF GOD'S FAITHFUL CHILDREN!

Why is it important that we understand **pre-advent judgment** to be a part of the Atonement? The answer is quite simple. Remember what happened to those in the Old Testament type who would not prepare for the Day Of Atonement? They were *"cut off from among his people,"* and God said, *"The same soul will I destroy . . ."* (Leviticus 23:29,30).

To those who have prepared and to those who are preparing for their record to be examined, the words of Revelation 22:12, carry special meaning. Look at it again: Jesus echoed, *"And, behold I come quickly; and My reward is with Me, to give every man according as his work shall be."*

May I ask a few personal questions? Are you ready for Jesus to come? Is He your Saviour? Will favorable judgment be passed in your behalf? Will you receive the reward of eternal life when He lays aside His High Priestly garments and puts on the clothing of "The King of kings and Lord of lords?"

Two boys were swimming when one became tired and began to scream, "Help! I'm drowning!" The other boy dove into the water and rescued his friend. The boys moved away from each other a short time later and grew to manhood. The one who almost drowned committed a crime and was brought to court to have his case presented. To his amazement, the judge was the friend who had rescued him from the would-be-watery grave. The guilty man stood in humiliation as the judge read the record and then spoke in a soft tine, "Many years ago I was your saviour and today I'm your judge."

Are you in need of forgiveness? Our Saviour-Judge is waiting to say, "You Are Forgiven."

Chapter Eleven

THE GATE OF EPHRAIM
and
THE PRISON GATE

"So the people went forth and brought them, and made themselves booths, every one upon the roof of his house, and in their courts, and in the courts of the house of God, and in the street of the water gate, and in the street of the ***gate of Ephraim*** *. . . And from above the gate of Ephraim, and above the old gate, and above the fish gate, and the tower of Hananeel, and the tower of Meah, even unto the sheep gate: and they stood still in the* ***prison gate****."*

(Nehemiah 8:16; 12:39)

The last two gates mentioned by Nehemiah are the **GATE Of EPHRAIM** and the **PRISON GATE**. It will be noted that there are no persons mentioned in connection with a construction process of these two gates, thus indicating that, in all likelihood, these two gates were not in need of repair. The spiritual lesson we gain is that: The course toward Glory will now have been completed and there will be nothing else human personalities can do as far as involvement in what will transpire thereafter. It will have all been settled.

The Spiritual Significance of the **GATE OF EPHRAIM** is that it **represents the Millennium.** Ephraim means "doubly fruitful."

The Spiritual Significance of the **PRISON GATE** is that it **represents the eternal safekeeping of the believer—the Golden Age.**

There have been some who have speculated as to what the Millennium and the Golden Age will be like, but since the Scriptures are not explicit as to many of the details (for a definite reason and purpose I am sure), it would be best for us to not allow our imagination to develop or promote ideas about things God has chosen not to reveal. *"The secret things belong unto the Lord our god: but those things which are revealed belong unto us and to our children forever"* (Deuteronomy 29:29).

There is much about the future we do not know, but of this we may be certain: Everything we need to enter eternity with the precious blood of Christ applied to our account has been revealed and God has made every provision for our future life; therefore, we should never endeavor to measure the conditions of the future life in Heaven and the New Earth by the conditions of this earthly life.

With this principle in mind and heart, let's notice some certainties relative to the **GATE OF EPHRAIM** and the **PRISON GATE**.

The Millennium (or 1,000 years) will be ushered in by the Second Coming Of Jesus, at which time John 14:2,3, will become a reality: *"In My* (Jesus is speaking) *Father's house are many mansions: if it were not so, I would have told you. I go to prepare a place for you. And if I go and prepare a place for you, I will come again, and receive you unto Myself; that where I am, there ye may be also."*

Revelation 20, contains a general portrait of what will happen in relation to the Millennium:

Satan will be bound in the bottomless pit.

Those who accepted Jesus as their Christ will love and reign with Him.

Those who refused to accept Jesus as their Christ will remain dead until the 1,000 years are finished.

At the end of the 1,000 years, Satan will be loosed for a little season in one final attempt to overthrow God's Kingdom.

At the end of the 1,000 years, Satan and the wicked will be cast into the lake of fire.

Revelation 21, 22, contain a general portrait of what will happen in relation to the Golden Age:

- A new heaven and a new earth will be established.
- New Jerusalem will become the Capital City of the new heaven and the new earth and the gates, walls, and foundations thereof will serve as a memorial to how God provided in the past and will provide and protect in all eternity.
- Eternal and intimate contact between God and His creation.
- Elimination of tears, death, sorrow, crying, pain, curse, and darkness.
- Availability to a pure river of water of life and the tree of life.

To say the least, as wonderful as the Christian life is now, **the best is yet to come**. Think about it. God invites us to be with Him in His provision – not just in this life, but for a 1,000 years after Jesus Returns – and not just for a 1,000 year Millennium, but for the Golden Age Of Eternity.

Two grand figures who were mightily used of God to point mankind unto to Messiah, reverberated the essence of this same Message Of Hope to their respective generations and to ours.

Isaiah – *"For since the beginning of the world men have not heard, nor perceived by the ear, neither hath the eye seen, O God, beside Thee what He hath prepared for him that waiteth for Him"* (Isaiah 64:4).

Paul – *"But as it is written, Eye hath not seen, nor ear heard, neither have entered into the heart of man, the things which God hath prepared for them that love Him"* (I Corinthians 2:9).

There are a couple of statements depicting the spirit of those who were in contact with these **two gates** that excite me in anticipation each time I read them.

After alluding to the **GATE OF EPHRAIM** (Nehemiah 8:16), the writer continues, *"And all the congregation of them that were* *come again out of the captivity made booths, and sat under the booths: for since the days of Jeshua the son of Nun unto that day had not the children of Israel done so.* ***And there was very GREAT GLADNESS****"* (verse 17).

Then after alluding to the **PRISON GATE** (Nehemiah 12:39), the writer continues, *"So stood the two companies of them that* ***gave thanks*** *in the house of God . . . Also that day* ***they*** *offered great sacrifices, and* ***rejoiced: for God had made them rejoice with GREAT JOY****: the wives also and the children rejoiced: so that the joy of Jerusalem was heard even afar off"* (verses 40,43).

To be sure, the gladness of Israel was great and their joy was heard even afar off, but as the old preacher once shouted, "you aint heard or seen nuthin' yet!" Indeed, the best is yet to come and God is eager for His children to inherit the provision of the Millennium and Golden Age with GREAT GLADNESS AND GREAT JOY.

When this takes place, then the Spiritual Significance of Nehemiah 12:39, will become a reality: ***". . . they stood still in THE PRISON GATE."***

Soon our journey will end and we will arrive in a better place – a place prepared just for us – a new heaven and a new earth. Then we will journey no more. We will stand still in awe of how wonderful God was to invite us to such a place and how patient He was as we encountered each of the steps along the path from earth to glory. Sometimes we stumbled, but He was always there to encourage us along the way.

PS

We have taken a marvelous trip together and as you close this book, it is my hope that the words of this manuscript have touched your mind and heart to awaken a greater desire than ever before to be a part of what yet awaits every child of God.

It is my desire that the closing prayer of Nehemiah might always be both my prayer and yours:

"Remember me, O my God, for good." **(Nehemiah 13:31)**

A M E N

Printed in the United States
52660LVS00002B/28-126

9 781424 141500